Managing School Crises
From Theory to Application

Barbara J. Ertl, MS, LPC, NCC

Dr. Mary Schoenfeldt

International Critical Incident Stress Foundation, Inc.

International Critical Incident Stress Foundation, Inc.
3290 Pine Orchard Lane, Suite 106
Ellicott City, MD 21042
USA
www.icisf.org

print ISBN: 978-0-9795692-2-7

eBook ISBN: 978-0-9795692-3-4

TABLE OF CONTENTS

OBJECTIVES
Participants will...

1. Describe the prevalence and outcomes of trauma exposure as reported in the ACE Study.

2. Describe the role of the National Incident Management system in the response to school crises.

3. Define the phases of a crisis event and how a CISM team can be involved in each.

4. Describe common reactions to traumatic events and how they can impact functioning in a school setting.

5. Explain the 6 Core Elements of CISM and how they can be utilized in responding to a traumatic event that impacts a school.

6. Describe the four CISM techniques most commonly utilized in a school setting.

7. Demonstrate, by participation in group exercises, an understanding of the informational group intervention process.

8. Demonstrate, by participation in role-plays, an understanding of the SAFER-R protocol and the interactive group protocols.

9. Explain the formula for strategic planning and how it can be utilized.

10. Describe the concept of suicide contagion and contributing factors to it.

SECTION ONE
THE NEED

Schools are safe but are the people in them safe? A quick internet search will reveal a multitude of events that have negatively impacted schools reaching back many decades, in the United States and across the world. **A quick sampling includes:**

05/18/1927	Bath (Michigan) School District bombing - 42 deaths
12/01/1958	Our Lady of the Angels School (Chicago) fire – 95 deaths
11/22/1963	Assassination of John F. Kennedy
08/01/1966	University of Texas massacre – 16 deaths
07/12/1976	California State University-Fullerton shooting – 7 deaths
01/19/1986	Space Shuttle Challenger Disaster
11/16/1989	East Coldingham (NY) Elementary School tornado – 7 deaths
1990's	51 separate school shootings in the US
04/19/1995	Oklahoma City bombing – Daycare Center – 18 deaths
03/13/1996	Dunblane Primary School (United Kingdom) – 17 deaths
09/11/2001	Terrorist attacks on the World Trade Center, Pentagon and a Shanksville
09/01/2004	Belsan (Russia) School massacre – 330 deaths
12/14/2012	Sandy Hook Elementary School shooting – 26 deaths
02/14/2018	Stoneman Douglas High School shooting – 17 deaths
03/26/2020	COVID-19 Pandemic

When people of any age are exposed to overwhelming events, they react in somewhat predictable ways. This training will explore the impact of events, specifically on students and school personnel, and how to best prepare for and respond to them. The primary focus of this training is directed at supporting students, preschool to 12th grade, and the faculty/staff who work in those buildings.

In 1998, a landmark study was published jointly by the Center for Disease Control (CDC) and Kaiser Permanente to look at the link between childhood trauma and adult health and well-being.

The Adverse Childhood Experiences (ACE) study looked at 10 indicators of trauma:

- Physical abuse

- Sexual abuse

- Emotional abuse

- Emotional neglect

- Physical neglect

- Alcohol or drug abuse in home

- Parental separation or divorce

- Depression or mental illness in home

- Mother treated violently

- Imprisoned household member

Results of the study include the following:

- Adverse Childhood Experiences are very common, approximately 2/3 of the population experienced at least 1 ACE prior to age 18, but are largely unrecognized.

- ACEs are strong predictors of death, disease, health risks, social functioning, well-being and medical care costs.

- ACEs are the basis for many major public health and social problems – including youth violence.

- ACEs are interrelated, not solitary. These combinations make ACEs the prime determinant of the health, social and well-being of our nation.

- There is a much higher prevalence of ACEs for those living in poverty.

Though interesting and having far–reaching implications for health and mental health cost, the ACE study is not comprehensive in its assessment of trauma-exposure in youth. For example, excluded from the study was any traumatic event that occurred outside of the home such as natural disasters (hurricanes, tornadoes, floods and wildfires) or man-made disasters (community violence, rioting, terrorism and bullying). Also, not included in the study were events that were highly publicized or transmitted via social media that could result in secondary traumatic stress. Therefore, though the results of the ACE Study may suggest that 60-80% of youth are exposed to a traumatic incident, in all likelihood, trauma exposure is almost a universal experience in some communities.

So why should school personnel care about trauma exposure in students and staff? The answer to that question is: because trauma impacts a person's ability to function (cognitively, emotionally and behaviorally) in the classroom and to fully engage in the learning process. Traumatic events hit people at a primitive level, resulting in psychological and physiological disequilibrium, and force people into survival mode. Simply put, if we want our students and staff to perform well in the school environment, then we need to support them through traumatic events.

SECTION TWO
STANDARD OF CARE
Legal and Ethical Requirements

School personnel often think the worst nightmare of their lives is if something happens on their campus that has caused physical damage, injuries and maybe even loss of life. 9-1-1 has been called and 35 emergency vehicles scream into the parking lot at a high rate of speed with lights and sirens blaring. It can't get any worse, can it? Unfortunately, it can and it does. It gets worse when police and fire have done their jobs... treating injured or investigating a crime. They pack up and leave. You watch them turn out their flashing lights, silence the sirens and very slowly leave your parking lot. You watch their tail lights slowly recede and realize it's now YOUR crisis. It's YOUR job to figure what to do next.

CISM, NIMS and ICS

Where does CISM fit in an overall school Emergency Operations Plan? How does it (or we) integrate into an Incident Command System? What Standards of Care should guide our efforts? These are the questions that surface both before and after a school crisis. As we evolve as an accepted and welcome piece of overall crisis management, the answers change. We learn each time someone somewhere responds to a crisis that impacts a school system. Sometimes it's a crisis at the school itself... an accident with a school bus on the way to school, an act of violence in a classroom, a natural death of a student or staff member. Crisis can visit your school from outside as well... an industrial accident in the community that injures or kills employees, a shooting at the local mall or movie theater, a natural disaster that threatens and then destroys portions of your town. After each, we look back and see what worked and what might need to be adjusted next time. With each of these, the response is critical and blends in with efforts at recovery. A common conversation when it's over is how did we support our staff and students and how can we do even better should we have to.

The standard model from FEMA and US Department of Education outlines the phases of Prevention, Mitigation, Protection, Response and Recovery. It is this authors' experience that there is yet another phase in every crisis... between Response and Recovery and that phase is CHAOS! This is the period of time when everything seems out of control, maybe the incident itself is managed... the fire is almost out, the students have been relocated to another location, the police are finishing their work and now the school team steps in to take over. It's a time you hope to remember where that school manual is that tells you what to do next. For most, the manual stays on the shelf for a while yet and people spring into action and take charge to do what needs to be done. Your school plan may include calling for counselors right away or involving community chaplains, Red Cross mental health volunteers or other groups to help calm and support students. Many communities now have integrated community CISM teams that may respond.

The challenge early on is to organize this corps of well intentioned, skilled and hopefully requested resources. It falls to the school to take charge of this from the start in order to know who is providing what service to which population. If left unchecked and uncoordinated, the risk is that someone will be missed who needs services or a group may be over run as we duplicate services. Or even worse, you have a 'Trauma Tourist' that is drawn to your crisis out of their own need and may or may not be appropriate to be with students. The final responsibility and liability will rest with the school system and it's best to take the lead from the beginning rather than try to corral the chaos later.

NIMS

In 2005, the Office of Homeland Security set out guidelines for NIMS, the National Incident Management System. This system is designed to enable a coordinated response among jurisdictions and agencies and establishes common processes for planning and managing resources. According to FEMA, NIMS provides a standardized, on-scene, all hazards integration of facilitates, equipment, personnel, procedures and communications within a common organizational framework.

A cornerstone of NIMS is the Incident Command System. This system is based on what needs to be done, not who does it. It's not based on titles and directions such as "The Principal will do..." instead it says "The Incident Coordinator will do..." In its simplest form, it is a system to coordinate all that needs to be done... in other words, it's just a structure for a committee and who is better at committees than schools? No one!

Incident Command Structure

The Incident Command System may be functioning on several levels at the beginning of the crisis. If the event is one that happens suddenly, involves injuries, a hazardous materials incident or a crime, the official first responders will assume overall command. The school incident command structure will coordinate with the community command and will act as a Liaison rather than as the Incident Commander. FEMA has an excellent updated on-line course on Incident Command System for Schools, IS100.SC-a which can be found at www.training.fema.gov.

Field Operations –Unified Command

Unified Command
Police   Fire   School
DC   AC   Sup

Liaisons   Safety

Staging Areas   PIO/JIS

Operations
Police   Fire   School
Capt.   BC   Rep

| Police Entry Group (Police Only) Hot Zone | Rescue Group (Police & Fire) Warm Zone | Medical Group (Fire Only) Cold Zone | School Branch |

Entry Teams (Police Only) Hot Zone

Extraction Teams (Police & Fire) Warm Zone

Rescue Teams (Police & Fire) Warm Zone

Triage (Fire Only) Cold Zone

Transport (Fire Only) Cold Zone

Treatment (Fire Only) Cold Zone

Everett Emergency Management

Reunification

Student, Staff accountability

Evacuation Shelter site

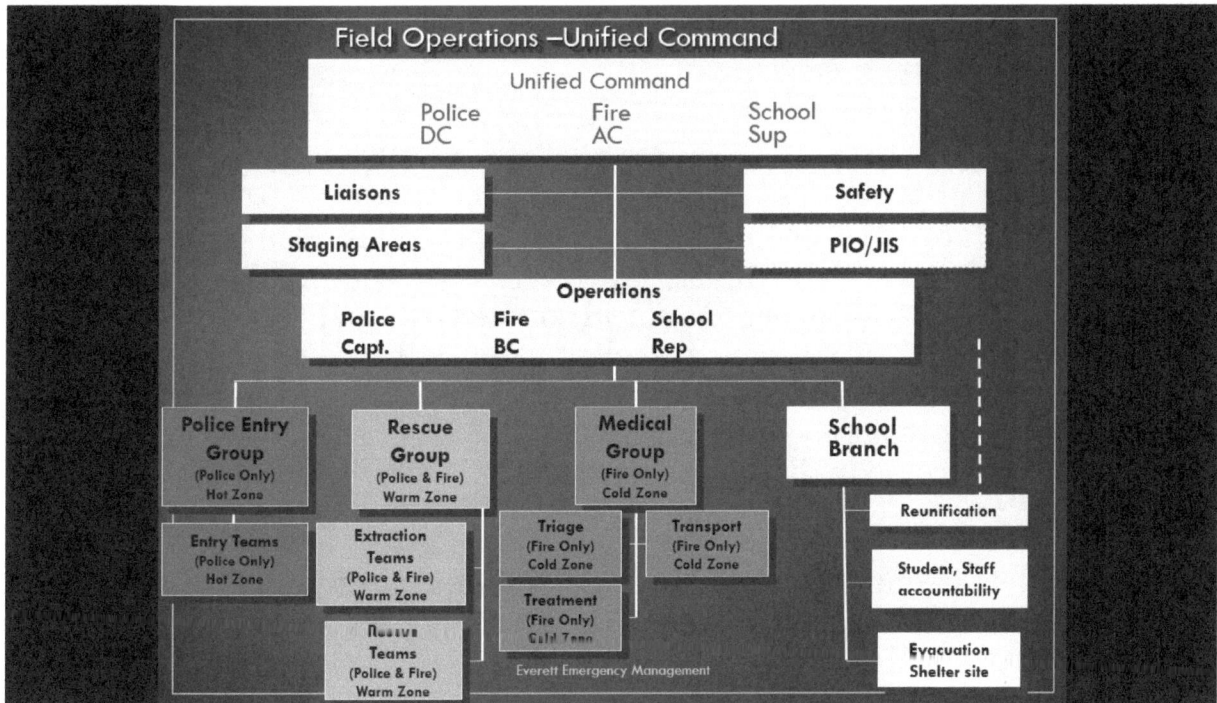

The above graphic is an example of where the school can connect into an overall Unified Command Structure for the initial response. It acknowledges that the school is the true first responder in any incident that happens on campus and as such, is the first command structure that is set up. Schools have already begun to respond with activities to protect the lives of students and have policies and procedures to guide them. They are an equal partner in the management of the incident and as such, a high level representative is a member of the Unified Command Structure and a site level staff is guiding and coordinating the actual campus response in partnership with fire or police. That may be through the Operations Section or possibly through the Liaison assignment.

Federal Guidance

Following the Sandy Hook shooting, amidst the outcry about gun violence, a new resource was created to coordinate and systemize school specific crisis response. President Barrack Obama created the Now Is the Time plan that included the development of a guide to assist schools and community responders plan for and respond to crisis affecting a school community. It drew on what was already in place and added new best practices. The document is called a Guide to Emergency Operations Plans and was jointly developed by the US Department of Education, Department of Justice, FBI, Homeland Security, FEMA, and Department of Health and Human Services. It was the first time these six agencies had collaborated on a project such as this. The result is a comprehensive document that outlines the format of a school Emergency Operations Plan and coordinates the language with first responders and others who might play a role in a crisis. You can find more information at www.rems.ed.gov.

School Emergency Operations Plan Basics

The basic structure of a School Emergency Operations Plan includes these components: The Basic Plan, Threat and Hazard Specific Annex (what do we do in an earthquake, or a violent act or a suicide on campus) and Functional Annexes (how do we evacuate, lockdown or shelter in place for instance). And most importantly to those of us who are part of a CISM program, Recovery. The plan for the first time looks at school crisis through the lens of before, during and after a crisis. This is mirrored in the planning to include before, during and after school activities.

The word Annex is one that is common among official responders but may be unfamiliar in a school setting. In this context, it is used in place of the word Appendix to describe the sections in a document.

The suggested Annexes include:

- Communication and Warning

- Evacuation

- Shelter in Place

- Accounting for All Persons

- Family Reunification

- Security

- Continuity of Operations

- Health: Public, Medical and Mental

- Recovery

The one we are most concerned with in this course is the annex specifically for Recovery and to a smaller extent, Health: Public, Medical and Mental. This is where our CISM team and services will fit. The guidance from the US Department of Education suggests the Recovery Annex focus on 4 primary areas:

- Academic

- Physical

- Fiscal

- Psychological – Emotional

At first glance it would seem our CISM program is only concerned with the last one, Psychological-Emotional. However, let's look more closely.

Academic

In the following chapter we will talk about the effects of trauma on the academic environment and how our efforts can make a difference. Academic performance and scores are most likely going to suffer while students and staff alike cope with the crisis. By providing CISM support, the hope is that the amount of time it takes to recover academically will be shortened.

Physical

Physical is referring to the facilities, the physical environment that students and staff are occupying following the crisis. Your CISM team can play a very valuable role when decisions are being made about the physical environment. Do we reopen school in its current condition or location? Do we remodel? And what about the empty desk in the classroom... do we take it out or leave it? Your team may coordinate a Crisis Management Briefing (CMB) to start to hear comments from the whole community about their thoughts and wishes. Another valuable service you provide is Administrative Guidance and Assessment as decisions are being made.

Fiscal

Fiscal is an area that you may or may not have input into although you may have important observations. A school shooting for instance that happens in a cafeteria will have several decisions attached to resuming the food service. It may be less expensive to feed everyone in the large gym while the cafeteria is being repaired or replaced but you understand the anxiety that large crowds may cause for students now so your input to look at fiscally appropriate small gathering spaces may be welcome.

Psychological – Emotional

The Psychological – Emotional section of the Recovery plan should not only outline the types of services and interventions you may provide, but also how you will coordinate those services, what resources are available to you and how you will access even more resources should you need them. And many times you will need additional resources. School crisis isn't resolved in a short time and our CISM support services should be available for the long haul.

When we dig deeper into our role as a CISM program during Recovery, as suggested by the US Department of Education, we see 4 new subcategories:

- Leadership
- Counseling
- Memorials
- Promotion of Coping and Support Resiliency

Leadership: Team Function

In essence, your team is a system within a much broader system. Your team itself is only a part of the CISM program that your school and/or your community has created. Your CISM program is only a part of the larger school or community system. Each segment has some autonomy but has to coordinate and collaborate with the other pieces. At times this will synchronize just like the Radio City Musical Hall Rockets and other times it will feel more like the Keystone Cops running in circle and bumping into each other!

You have your own:

- recruitment processes

- training requirements

- call out procedures

- team leadership development plan

- logistics coordinator

- team support and debriefing protocol

- collaborative partnerships with other school or community CISM teams

- compassion fatigue management system

Crisis Intervention and Counseling

CISM programs will spend much of their planning and training time getting ready to be called. An effective program has a training plan to bring new members into not only response positions but team leadership positions. The overall plan will include how to address the immediate, short term and long term needs of the entire school community... students, staff and parents. The types of activities may change over time but the underlying purpose does not. That purpose being to provide a supportive, educational environment that helps people as they work to make sense out of the senseless. Your program also includes screening for further interventions as well as the partnerships and procedures to access those more intense services should you need them.

Commemorations and Memorials

Planning includes how you handle memorials of all types. Whether those are physically on or off a school site, temporary or permanent, paper... cards, signs, drawing... gifts from well-wishers, even slide shows and videos. Memorials and commemorations come in many forms and the time to plan how to handle them is before they become an emotionally laden time bomb. It's much easier to say to a grieving parent who wants the statue in front of your school to commemorate their child who was killed in an accident in the parking lot that you are sorry for their loss but you simply cannot do that. You have a policy and procedure concerning memorials that include a respectful timeframe, can only be temporary and not on school property or in a location that interferes with students or staff.

Examples of Respectful and Effective Memorial Ideas

- Following a school shooting, the fence along the front perimeter of the school was designated at the Remembrance Fence. The word memorial indicates permanence and was deliberately not used. A district leader found a small teddy bear and put it in the weave of the fence, that acted as a magnet for others to add to it. It was known the fence would be used as a place to remember and grieve and would have supportive staff and community members there most of the time. The school staff also watched and removed anything that was distasteful or inappropriate as well as wilted flowers and rain soaked paper. At the suggestion of the CISM team, the school put together a small group that included a staff member, students, victim's families and city parks department to plan how the items on the fence would be removed when the time was up. The timing was planned and everyone was notified several times of the upcoming date. A date was set that was approximately 1 month from the incident. As the time to disassemble the fence came near, families were invited to come privately and take anything they wished, students and staff were invited to help remove all the items during a lunch period if they wanted to help. Plans were made to sort the items into what was compostable so it could be recycled and returned to the school the next year in the landscaping, what could be burned in an approved ceremonial bon fire and what would be thrown away. Media was invited and controlled through a Public Information Officer on scene. The message through media was this fence was like a sympathy card you put on the mantle after Grampa dies. It was never meant to be a permanent display but was instead a way to acknowledge the loss, honor the victims and move forward.

- Another example is the use of a small blank journal or scrapbook to eventually be given to a family member of the victim. A CISM team member brings one and lets the school community know of its existence. The message is that it will be on campus for a specified length of time... say 2 weeks. Students and staff are encouraged to add notes including favorite memories, maybe photos and words of condolences for the family. After 2 weeks, the notebook is taken out of circulation on campus. Someone reads the entire book just to be sure comments and pictures won't bring further pain to the family. The book is then taken to the family by a CISM member or leader from the school. This method gives students and staff a forum to express their grief and reactions and also gives the message that yes, we care, yes we hurt, and as a school community, we will move forward and not stay in the initial intensity forever.

Those are just two examples of how the CISM team can guide memorials and remembrances in ways that are respectful and appropriate.

Community/school grief is different from family grief and without careful preplanning and management, a school can get caught in the intensity of family grief and not know how to extract themselves without hard feelings, confusion and more pain.

Standard of Care

As with any profession, CISM programs and team members should adopt and follow a Standard of Care. At the very least, the Standard of Care should address Confidentiality, Culture Competence, Self-Care, Compassion Fatigue Management, and Continuing Education. The resource chapter has two samples addressing Traumatologists and Mental Health Professionals and can serve as suggestions and guidance as you develop your own.

Conclusion

The legal, ethical and practical requirements for an effective CISM program come from many organizations and directions. CISM is listed on the SAMSHA National Registry of Evidence Based Programs and Practices. The inclusion of CISM services are reflected in guidance, and in some cases regulations, from Federal, State, Regional and Local jurisdictions. CISM teams have been in place in schools and communities around the world for many years and have performed invaluable services to countless students, staff and families.

A Life Changing Experience

By Barb Ertl, MS NCC, LPC

The school year of 1997-98 proved memorable for 4 high profile school shootings. The year began with the shooting in Pearl, Mississippi, followed 3 months later by one in West Paducah, Kentucky. In April of 1998, the third school shooting of the year occurred in Edinboro, Pennsylvania and the final one happened in Springfield, Oregon in May.

I was personally involved in the Edinboro response for 17 months following that event. At the time, I was the crisis team leader for the regional educational agency that supported that school district so, my involvement began within hours of the actual shooting. The incident was small in comparison to a Columbine or Sandy Hook as it involved the murder of 1 teacher and the wounding of 3 middle school students. However, it occurred in a small, rural town where few people locked their doors as crime of any kind was something that happened miles away in the "city".

I learned many lessons about supporting students, parents, faculty members and the community at large as the members of the school district crisis team and my agency's crisis team worked together to stabilize them. Very long days and evenings for weeks on end stretched the resources and tolerance of team members almost to the breaking point, but still there was work to be done if healing were to occur.

Throughout my time with that school district and with many others since, I have always relied on the knowledge and skills that I had gained through multiple CISM trainings. It was in 1992 that I first became acquainted with the CISM model of crisis intervention. At that time, I had been approached by a colleague of mine who was also a deputy fire chief with a volunteer fire department. In that capacity, he and his fellow firefighters and EMTs had been pressed in to action to respond to a series of completed suicides; these were of neighbors, relatives and other people known to the first responders. My colleague described the toll that these calls had taken on his personnel which included a failure to respond to calls. His department was thus impaired and this deputy chief was looking for assistance to help them heal from the traumatic events they had been responding to in their community. Together, he and I went to a CISM training, brought it back to his department and the healing began.

Little did I realize that that experience would have a major impact on me both personally and professionally. Personally, I wound up joining that fire department and became a firefighter, EMT and fire police officer. I responded to calls during days, nights, weekends and holidays for 18 years. It was a great experience.

However, it was my exposure to, and experience with, CISM that has defined my professional life. From 1992 forward, I consistently integrated the CISM structure and protocols into all crisis responses that I was called to in the 12 - school district response area that my agency supported. Little did I realize that when it came to the Edinboro

18

school shooting, my training in CISM would prove to be pivotal in both the response but also in the criminal proceedings for the perpetrator of the crime. Obviously, the strategic planning and intervention protocols were used throughout the event. However, it was at a court hearing that all of that proved invaluable.

I had been subpoenaed to testify in the hearing to determine if the 14-year-old perpetrator should be tried as a juvenile or as an adult. In introducing me to the courtroom, the prosecuting attorney asked me my name, role and credentials. He then asked me to describe what training I had, specifically in crisis intervention, and how I could be sure that what I had been doing in the school was not causing harm. I related my training in CISM and cited some of the research. The school psychologist who led the district crisis team testified after me. He was asked the same questions, but though he had a doctorate in psychology and 30 years of experience, he was forced to admit that he had no specific training in crisis intervention. It was after that experience that I realized that the bar had been raised for all members of school crisis teams.

The work that we do when we respond to crisis events can have profound effects on the lives of others. If we accept the responsibility of serving on a crisis team, we also accept the responsibility to know what to do, when, and how. The CISM model provides the structure and skills to do that and, though we will predictably be challenged by unpredictable situations, the lessons learned will continue to be integrated into best practice. The CISM model has evolved over 30 years and will continue to do so. And attorneys will continue to challenge us to raise the bar regarding our training, skills and competence.

Barbara J. Ertl, MS, LPC, NCC & Dr. Mary Schoenfeldt

SECTION THREE
PSYCHOTRAUMATOLOGY

When we support those impacted through CISM activities we educate about the impacts of crisis and trauma. In addition, we take away the stigma of a variety of reactions. We adjust not only the expectations but the methods of teaching following a crisis. As a result we have a better chance of resuming academic success.

Kids and Trauma: Implications for the Classroom

Much has been written about the effect of trauma and crisis on the primary areas of everyday functioning. Those areas are; emotional, physical, cognitive, behavioral and spiritual. Our children face an additional challenge by adding developmental stages to the mix. A crisis that affects children, whether that is something that happens at school or in the community can have profound impacts for all of us. We can look at the crisis through several sets of experiences and see a variety of reactions and implications.

In general, responses fall within the four primary areas of everyday functioning. Keep in mind some people, children and adults, may exhibit these typical reactions while others do not.

Emotional

Emotional reactions can span the spectrum:

- Sadness, depression and anxiety

- Anger and irritability

- Numb, withdrawn, or disconnected

- Feeling a lack of involvement or enjoyment in favorite activities

- Crying spells, hysteria

With children in a school setting, these can be confusing and challenging for the student to understand and the staff to manage. A student who is feeling sad and depressed may take more time than usual to get to class. A student who is feeling angry as an emotional reaction to a crisis may threaten a teacher or become disruptive in class. The student that feels a sense of hopelessness about the future sees no reason to even attend school let alone engage in educational activities.

Now let's talk about the adults... those parents and staff who want to do the best to support their children and re-engage them in a healthy experience of school. Adults can experience similar emotional reactions as children. The teacher who is feeling numb, withdrawn and disconnected is going to have a difficult time in their classroom as they work to stimulate thinking and even follow a simple lesson plan. If the Administrator of the school feels a lack of enjoyment or involvement in the profession that used to be exciting, their leadership decisions may be affected.

Physical

Physical reactions can take many forms:

- Sleep difficulties

- Gastrointestinal problems (diarrhea, cramps)

- Stomach upset, nausea

- Elevated heart rate

- Elevated blood pressure

- Elevated blood sugar

- With extended stress, suppression of immune system functioning

When students don't sleep well at night, it's next to impossible to be mentally awake enough to learn. Those with physical ailments such as stomach upset and headache may spend more time in the health room than in the classroom. Eventually for some, the flu may strike particularly hard or a cold will last exceptionally long because their immune system simply can't fight any longer.

The adults may have nightmares, or to avoid the nightmares and intrusive memories they may simply stay up much too late and avoid going to bed until the early morning. Or they have an extra glass or two of wine thinking it may help them sleep. When the alarm goes off for another day at work, it's nearly impossible to get up and be ready to face another challenging day knowing students will look to the adults for strength, support and guidance. Following a school crisis, it's not unusual for staff to have medical issues surface that can be at the very least be painful and inconvenient and at the worst, life threatening.

Cognitive

Cognitive reactions can make it difficult to learn:

- Difficulty concentrating

- Difficulty with memory

- Intrusive memories

- Recurring dreams or nightmares

- Difficulties with problem-solving

- Inability to understand consequence of behavior

School is the place students come to learn. But when the ability to learn is changed due to a traumatic event, it's heartbreaking. Learning requires the brain and all the senses to work together to perform a highly complex series of tasks that require concentration, memory, creative problem solving skills, and much like a computer, an operating system that can coordinate, file and sequence the information. Crisis or trauma can change not only the will to learn, but the actual ability to learn. When a student has difficulty concentrating because their brain cannot stay focused for more than a few seconds or when hearing a sound outside, or glancing at a picture on the wall or hearing a chair scrape the floor brings intrusive memories flooding back, it's impossible to hear the words being spoken about a geometry lesson. A high school girl who lost her best friend in a car accident talked about sitting in a classroom and looking at the teacher. She said, "I could see her, but I couldn't understand a word she was saying. It was like someone turned the volume all the way down."

The teacher who tries to teach when their own attention is elsewhere will have a hard time engaging students in a lesson or a conversation. What the teacher planned yesterday may be forgotten today. Or the background information on a well-loved topic may be jumbled when the teacher tries to tell a story to illustrate a teaching point. Added to this is the sheer exhaustion from trying to be strong for everyone else. It's no wonder teachers struggle to know how best to do their jobs following a crisis. And their jobs are to not only teach, but be the emotional pillar for students. Many do their best and then retire early or transfer to another school.

Behavioral

Behavioral reactions can be challenging and baffling for everyone, even those who are acting out.

- Fighting

- Substance abuse

- Being overprotective of family or friends

- Keeping excessively busy

- Isolating oneself from others or clinginess

- Being very alert at times, startling easily

- Avoiding places, activities, or people that bring back memories

Following a crisis, discipline referrals for students can skyrocket. Students who have never acted out before may be testing limits, or engaging in risky behavior. Those who already use what some consider unhealthy coping mechanisms or have few skills in handling stress, may find themselves in even more trouble at school. Adolescents, in particular, often cope with crisis reactions by engaging in higher risk activities... increased substance use, risky sex, and reckless driving are not uncommon. It's a way to break through the emotional numbing and also may be a way to express their new found realization that their world isn't as predictable as they believed. For some, suicide ideation will surface and the high risk behavior may become a practice or an outlet. Students may have a hard time concentrating due to hyper startle reactions to any noise or distraction. Other students may become withdrawn and isolate themselves from friends, family and familiar activities.

Adults may have similar reactions to children. For adults however, we can add food, gambling and shopping to the list of risky or unhealthy behaviors. Each is a way to try to regain control and cope. The food and increased use of alcohol may also have to do with the physiological release of chemicals to help manage stress. The chemicals released automatically may tell the body it needs sugar and carbohydrates to help cope. Under stress, most people don't crave carrots and apples, it's more likely chocolate and salted peanuts or donuts! Adults, like young people, might also have a difficult time with anger and frustration which can lead to arguments, disagreements and result in family problems including physical and emotional abuse.

Spiritual (Worldview)

Spiritual reactions are often overlooked but may include the following:

- Loss of meaning

- Loss of direction

- Needing to prove oneself

- Looking for magical fixes

- Questioning/loss of faith

- Loss of trust

Though reactions in this area may be experienced by children of any age, they may prove to be especially problematic during two stages of development. First and foremost is the loss of trust during the primary school years when children are most dependent upon adults to protect them. Failure to address this may result in years of insecurity and anxiety. Additionally, the spiritual domain is prominent during adolescents, a period in which teens are focusing on identity development (e.g. career, relationships, values, etc.) failure to mediate these reactions may results in aimlessness and social isolation.

Adults too can have significant reactions in this domain regardless of their age. However, it is imperative to attend to this as teachers and other staff members may question their competence and commitment to their profession and/or roll within the school.

Academic Challenges

The challenges to the school system and all its members... students, staff and family, can be daunting. In order to move towards rebalancing and recovery ... including academic success... the first step is to recognize what's happening to the ability to think, reason and learn. According to the National Child Traumatic Stress Network, children who have experienced complex trauma may have problems thinking clearly, reasoning and problem solving. And what does it take for a student to be successful academically? The ability to think clearly, reason and solve problems. Add to that list the ability to concentrate and remember. These all are often compromised by the emotional impact of a school crisis and it can be a recipe for frustration and failure if not recognized and managed.

The Brain

The brain is a marvelous, highly complex organ and works over time to protect us from harm and ensure our survival... whether the threat is physical or emotional. As a reaction to a crisis or trauma, our brains compartmentalize information into whatever it needs to manage the overload of stimulus. It activates the area that will be most useful for survival and slows down the functions of the higher-level thinking areas. In other words, it shuts down some functions and ramps up others with no input from our rational selves. For instance, a crisis or trauma sharpens our ability to focus on what's directly in front of us but can stop our ability to process other information. As an illustration, put your hand up to your face, as close as you can without touching. If you are asked what is the biggest thing you see in the room, you most likely will say your hand. From your perspective that's reality, but that doesn't mean the book, the desk, walls, the other people went away. You just can't see them or focus on them. Your brain is doing what it is meant to do... take in information, sort it in a way that it feels is the most helpful for you in any given situation and provide you with the abilities it believes you need to survive.

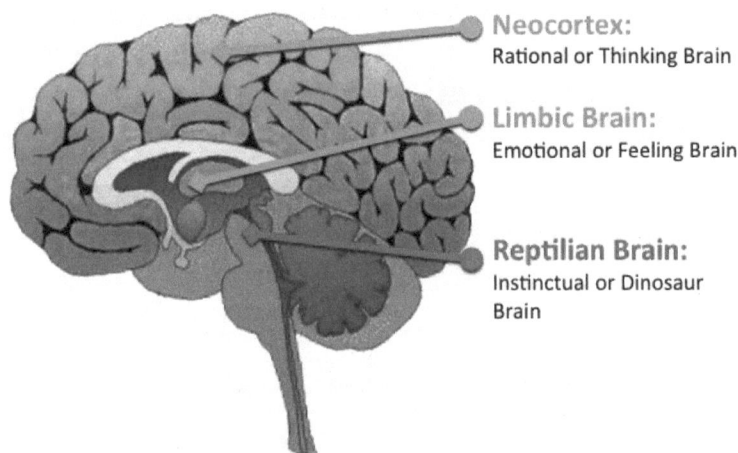

Neocortex:
Rational or Thinking Brain

Limbic Brain:
Emotional or Feeling Brain

Reptilian Brain:
Instinctual or Dinosaur Brain

When we experience trauma or crisis that includes fear, as sophisticated as the brain might be, it still believes the dinosaur may be chasing you and reacts accordingly to ensure your survival. It tells your physiological system to release the chemical that gives you a burst of speed, or the one that narrows your peripheral vision or the one that blots out memory of unimportant things... like where your keys might be or the name of the person you are talking with. The brain also triggers the physical responses of stomach upset or lack of bladder control.

After all you need to rid yourself of every ounce of unnecessary bulk so you can run faster from that dinosaur behind you. Your heart rate needs to increase so you can pump more blood to move more oxygen around, who cares if the blood pressure goes way out of control? What the brain doesn't understand though, is that the dinosaurs are gone and you really need to have your full cognitive ability in the days and weeks following a crisis. But you don't have them, you may not be able to concentrate, or solve even simple problems, or make a decision or mange your emotions or use good judgement. That is just the reality of crisis.

Whether you are 6 or 16 or 46, the brain and the body will be impacted by a crisis or trauma. Some reactions will fade quickly, others may take longer. For most, awareness, support and at times simple intervention and education will be enough to prevent lifelong ramifications. It's important to have community mental and behavioral health providers as strong partners to help support, screen and treat those who have experienced crisis. Effective early intervention is a collaboration between CISM teams and specialized mental and behavioral health providers.

The Staff

Staff reactions can come in many forms. For some, it will mean dragging themselves to school when they are exhausted, overwhelmed, ill or simply unable to fully function. But they will do it anyway, after all, the students need them. For others, it may be almost impossible to force themselves to come to school. Following a highly publicized school shooting, at least one staff member would sit in the car in the parking lot before school and call a retired psychologist friend and start the conversation with "I know they need me and are waiting for me, but I just am not sure I can do it today". The friend would simply listen while the staff member gathered their strength and resolve for one more day.

At another school, following a particularly horrific crisis, one staff wrote an email to the Superintendent. It said, "Please don't open school tomorrow, I'm not ready. I'm ok myself, but I worry about the students who have been so emotionally wounded. I can't stand to see their faces, hear their sobs and feel their pain. What do I say to them? How can I help them? I feel so helpless. This isn't what I went to college to do and I'm not up to it. But if you decide to open school, I will be there. I have to, it's my job and they need me."

When we support those impacted through CISM activities, educate about the impacts of crisis and trauma, take away the stigma of a variety of reactions and adjust not only the expectations but the methods we use to teach, we have a better chance of resuming academic success. Remember, it's not only students who have had a crisis impact their lives, it's the adults also. The teacher trying to teach a room full of students following a crisis may not be the same as they were just prior to the crisis any more than the students are the same.

Possible Actions to Recovery:

- Adjust curriculum but keep structure and appropriate expectations

- Adjust classroom content to adjust to shorter attention spans and inability to concentrate or problem solve.

- Support teaching staff by providing on going CISM activities to help them vent and learn coping strategies for their own reactions

- If possible, adjust curriculum to activities that are simple to teach and facilitate to help the staff be successful.

- Provide ongoing support to staff through Employee Assistance Programs or community mental health networks

- Provide ongoing support to students through Student Assistance Programs and School Based Support Groups.

- Suicide ideation can be a common reaction for some people… students and staff alike. Bring in a Suicide Prevention program, training and strategy. It not only increases competence, but also confidence that may have been shaken by the crisis. A strong word of caution however, always couple suicide education with having suicide prevention resources available and visible and long term.

- Help staff recover by providing educational information on Compassion Fatigue and Resilience. The US Department of Education has an excellent training and other resources on the Resilient Educator through the REMS Technical Assistance Center. www.rems.ed.gov.

- Begin Parenting Programs. The more parents are educated and understand what's happening with their children, the more reassured they will be and the better able to support themselves, the school and their children.

Post Traumatic Growth

A topic we don't hear enough about is Post Traumatic Growth. We know trauma impacts people and we are all familiar with the term Post Traumatic Stress. An actual diagnosis of Post-Traumatic Stress Disorder includes identifying symptoms that interfere with critical relationships and functions and have lasted more than 1 month.

Post Traumatic Growth however is what can happen when someone experiences a life changing event, a crisis, and comes out the other side stronger, more aware and more engaged in life. For the person themselves, that may mean a reprioritizing of life, a new found realization of just how strong they are that they were able to get through something they felt was unbearable, and an interest in issues that now have more meaning to them. It can result in stronger relationships, new confidence and new skills. For the school staff member, it might even mean leaving the field of education to pursue another career. Some staff leave out of exhaustion, those who are experiencing Post Traumatic Growth may leave out of strength. The school system or community may also reflect Post Traumatic Growth with new partnerships, new programs and a refocus on priorities. Post Traumatic Growth is the up side of the crisis coin and one we need to acknowledge and encourage.

Conclusion

The impact of crisis is profound and varied. It changes lives forever in ways we can never anticipate. When everyone in a school community recognizes the impacts and works together to educate and support, it makes a difference. CISM activities are an integral part of a complex response system that addresses the reactions of students and adults alike.

SECTION FOUR
CRITICAL INCIDENT STRESS MANAGEMENT INTERVENTION TECHNIQUES

There are many models of crisis interventions that may, and have been utilized, in schools. These include ones developed by the National Organization of Victim Assistance (NOVA), the National Association of School Psychologists (NASP) and the International Critical Incident Stress Foundation (ICISF-CISM). In addition, some schools utilize stand-alone crisis intervention techniques (e.g. Psychological First Aid, comfort rooms) as a one-size-fits-all remedy to crisis.

It is important to recognize the goals of crisis intervention:

- stabilize the situation and the person

- normalize reactions to the crisis

- mobilize coping skills and supports

- assess functioning

It is also important to remember that crisis intervention techniques that have been developed for individuals may not be effective with groups and vice versa. Thus the need for specialized training for crisis intervention is needed to avoid doing harm.

Critical Incident Stress Management (CISM) is a comprehensive, integrated, systematic and multi-component model of crisis intervention that was first developed by Dr. Jeffrey Mitchell and Dr. George Everly beginning in 1973. It has been utilized with many diverse populations throughout the United States and many other countries throughout the world. The school curriculum has been taught since 2000.

Generally speaking, once the school/district has created the infrastructure for good crisis management (e.g. policies/procedures, plan and team), it is time to provide the team members with specific training in crisis intervention techniques.

The CISM Model of crisis intervention includes 6 Core Elements.
They are:

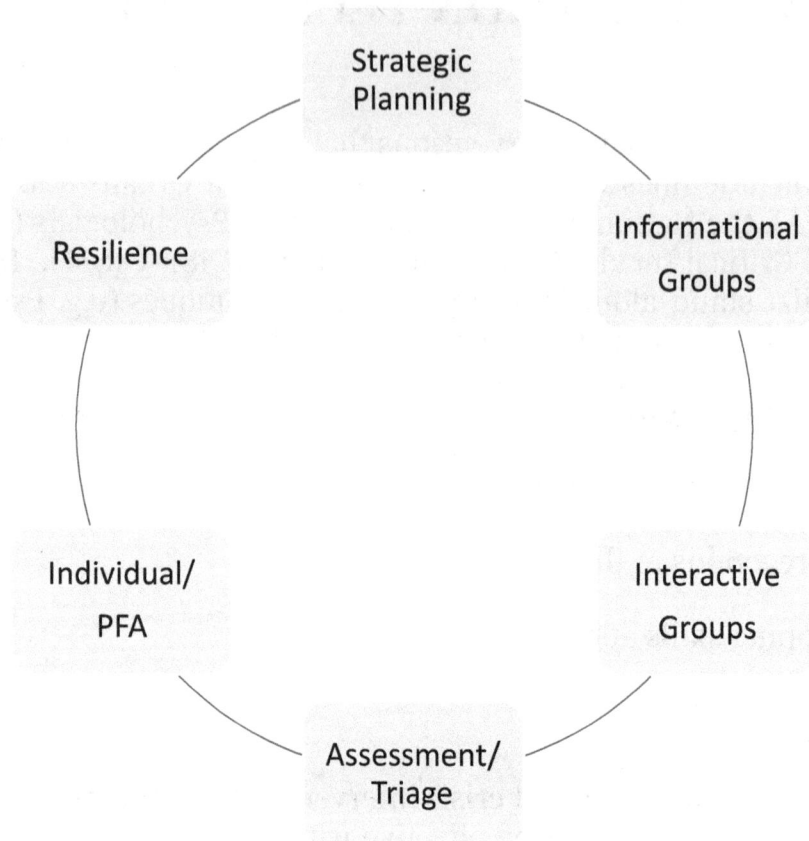

1. Strategic Planning

2. Informational Group Crisis Intervention – Crisis Management Briefings

3. Interactive Groups – Defusings and CISD

4. Assessment and Triage

5. Individual Crisis Intervention – SAFER-R

6. Fostering Personal and Community Resilience

Individual Crisis Intervention Protocol

The most common crises that school personnel need to deal with occur on an individual basis. Examples of an individual crisis might include: death of a family member, being the victim of an assault or other crime, or exposure to child abuse. In these circumstances, utilization of the SAFER-R protocol may be used to assist the person in crisis. The protocol includes the following steps:

SAFER – Revised

Stabilize (introductions, meet basic needs, mitigate acute stressors)

Acknowledge the crisis (listen to their story and reactions)

Facilitate understanding (normalize their reactions)

Encourage effective coping (self-care, installation of hope)

Restore or **R**efer (facilitate access to care-informal or formal)

Individual crisis intervention can be done at any time, provided there is a safe and private location, adequate time to work through the protocol and a person that has been trained to apply it. It does not require a mental health clinician to utilize this technique.

Exercise: SAFER-R
Observation Form

Describe 3 observations in each phase:

Stabilize:

Acknowledge:

Facilitate:

Encourage:

Restore or Refer:

Were the transitions between phases smooth or natural?

Were the steps followed in order?

Comments:

Informational Group Intervention Protocol

Not all crises occur on an individual basis and thus additional crisis intervention techniques are necessary to respond to other types of tragedies. Within the Critical Incident Stress Management model there are two types of group interventions. These are: informational groups and interactional groups; both can be utilized within the school setting.

The informational group, also known as a **Crisis Management Briefing (CMB)** is designed to begin the stabilization process for small groups (individual classrooms, faculty groups, teams) or large groups (student body, parents, community members) that have been affected by a crisis. These groups need not be homogenous in terms of their level of impact and CMBs can be held at any point that there is a need to convey new information to a group of people. A Crisis Management Briefing can be especially powerful in setting the tone for subsequent intervention activities.

A Crisis Management Briefing is always conducted by at least 2 people. In a school setting they are typically conducted by a school administrator and another member of the crisis team such as a school psychologist, counselor or social worker.

The 4 steps of a CMB are as follows:

> **Step1:** Assemble the participants
>
> **Step 2:** Present the facts re: crisis situation
>
> **Step 3:** Discuss and normalize common reactions
>
> **Step 4:** Discuss coping strategies and available resources.
>
> *Optional:* question and answer period

For large events, or those that are ongoing (e.g. school shooting with subsequent criminal proceedings), it may be necessary to provide multiple Crisis Management Briefings over time. CMBs can also be given via radio or television.

Interactional Group Intervention Protocols

Most events that impact a school do so at varying levels and so additional support beyond a Crisis Management Briefing may be needed. In determining what interventions may be indicated, several factors need to be assessed.

These include:

- number of people affected
- level of impact
- access to the individuals
- size and training of the response team
- follow-up and referral resources

When an incident affects more than 3 students and/or staff members, oftentimes it is both more effective and efficient to provide support services in groups. To do this, it is critical to determine their level of impact. Level of impact can be conceptualized by using a bulls-eye with the inner circle representing those directly involved in the event and subsequent circles representing proximity (physical or relational) to those involved in the event. (However, care must be taken in determining which group a person is included in so as not to further traumatize them.)

Example: 2-vehicle accident

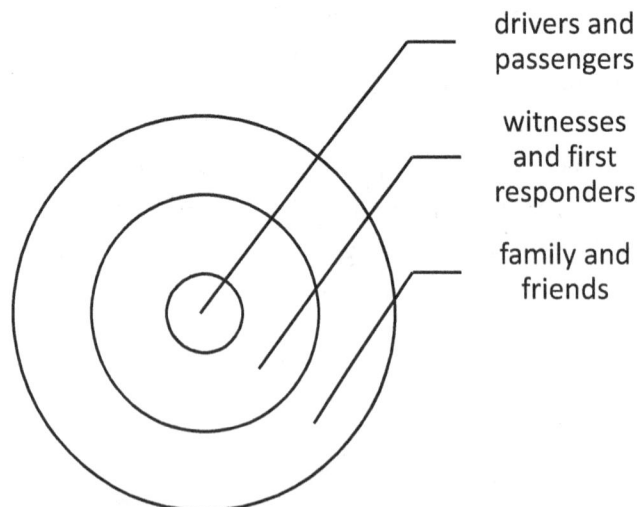

drivers and passengers

witnesses and first responders

family and friends

The interactional group crisis intervention techniques utilized in Critical Incident Stress Management incorporate the 10 healing factors identified by Irvin Yalom in effective groups.

These include:

1. impart information

2. instill hope

3. altruism

4. universal concepts

5. corrective recapitulation

6. using socializing techniques

7. initiate behaviors

8. interpersonal learning

9. group cohesiveness

10. catharsis

Research suggests that there is a dose-response relationship to trauma. Thus, in triaging the response to an event, priority should be given to those with the most exposure to the event (as represented by the innermost circle) as access to them becomes available. Once the level of impact is determined and access is given to an individual, the school crisis team can then begin to assign impacted students to interactive intervention groups.

There are 2 types of interactive intervention groups: defusing and the Critical Incident Stress Debriefing (CISD). The defusing process is designed to stabilize a traumatized group and to facilitate the assessment of the group members to determine what other services may be needed. Additional goals for a defusing are: to mitigate the impact of the traumatic event, reduce the cognitive, emotional and physiological symptoms and accelerate the recovery process.

Defusings

Defusings are most effective if done within 8-12 hours of the event. They are facilitated by at least 2 people who are trained to do them. In schools, a teacher, coach or advisor may be included in the group to assist with assessing students but should not be a participant in the same group with students. Once a particular group is identified as homogenous by level of impact and available for a defusing, they are gathered in a quiet, comfortable and private location to begin the process.

The defusing process consists of 3 phases:

>**Phase 1:** Introduction
>
>**Phase 2:** Exploration
>
>**Phase 3:** Information

During the **Introduction phase**, the following topics are discussed:

- introduction of the facilitators

- purpose of the meeting - provide support to the group

- indicate that it will last approximately 30 minutes

- set age appropriate rules for participants

- discuss confidentiality

- inform participants that participation is voluntary

- describe the questions to be asked

- assure participants that no notes are kept regarding content

- inform participants that this is not part of an investigation

- offer individual support after the session

During the **Exploration phase**, the following occurs:

- participants are asked to give a brief description of the event from their point of view and initial reaction to it <u>or</u>

- participants not directly involved in the incident are asked how they heard about and what they know about the event

- the facilitators ask clarifying questions but do not probe for details

- facilitators monitor participants for signs of distress and the need for individual support after the defusing

During the **Information Phase**, the following are discussed:

- summarize key points of the incident

- normalization of reactions

- anticipation of distress remitting over time

- coping strategies

- instillation of hope

Defusings are helpful with beginning the process of recovery from a traumatic event. They often are used in combination with other intervention techniques (e.g. individual crisis intervention or CISD) but for some groups they are sufficient for healing. Within the school setting, monitoring by teachers and other school personnel is strongly encouraged.

Exercise: Defusing

Describe 3 observations in each phase:

Introduction:

Exploration:

Information:

Were the transitions between phases smooth and natural?

Were the steps followed in order?

Were the questions clearly stated?

Comments:

Critical Incident Stress Debriefing

The second, and more intense, interactive group intervention is the **Critical Incident Stress Debriefing (CISD)**. It is designed to be:

- used with homogenous groups

- used 1-10 days after the event or when psychologically ready

- used with an ideal group size of 3 -20 participants

- facilitated by at least 2 CISM-trained people, <u>one of whom is a mental health clinician</u>

- 1-3 hours in length dependent upon the timing and age of participants

- confidential in nature

- voluntary

When organizing a CISD, much planning and preparation is required. For instance, because a Critical Incident Stress Debriefing may last an hour or more, care must be given to when in the course of a school day it is held so as not to interfere with lunch periods or dismissal times. Location is another concern when organizing a CISD. It should be held in a quiet place with limited access, but in a venue that is comfortable for the participants. Chairs should be arranged in a circle format, if at all possible, to allow the facilitators an opportunity to clearly observe the body language of the participants. Occasionally, CISDs are held in the classroom setting. If this is the case, then care must be given to the placement of the facilitators so as not to give the impressions of "talking at" the participants.

Critical Incident Stress Debriefings follow a 7-step process with 3 exceptions. These exceptions will be delineated later in this chapter. The 7-step process is designed to systematically engage the participant at a cognitive (less threatening) level, move to a more affective (more vulnerable) level and then return them back to a more cognitive level of processing the event. Thus, it is important that the steps of the CISD be followed in order and that no breaks be given during it and that it be completed in a single sitting.

COGNITIVE

INTRODUCTION   RE-ENTRY

FACT   TEACHING

THOUGHT   SYMPTOM

REACTION

AFFECTIVE

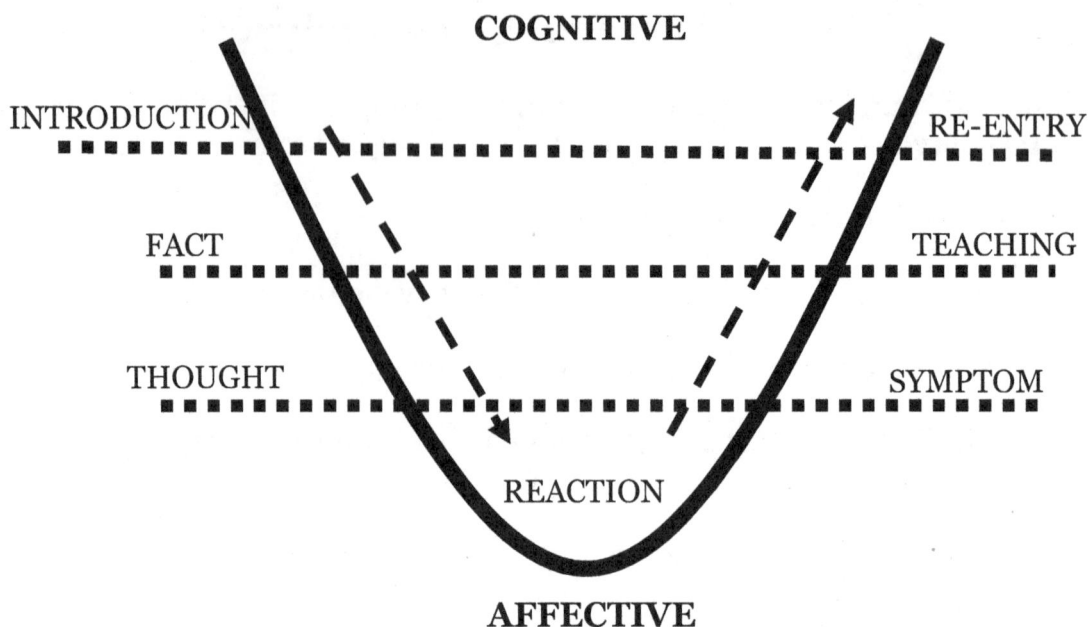

Introduction: -identify and introduce the facilitators

-describe purpose of the meeting

-discuss confidentiality/limits of confidentiality

-set age appropriate rules

-discuss voluntary participation, right to pass

-no breaks

-not psychotherapy

-preview questions to be asked in next step

*Note: for the fact and thought phases of the CISD, participants are asked to go around the circle to answer the questions. This is used to motivate and prepare the participants to engage in the process.

Fact: -identify who participant is and how connected to the event

-discuss "subjective reality" = understanding of the event

Thought: -identify first or most prominent thought once the reality of event becomes known

-follow-up for assessment purpose "what are current thoughts about the situation"

Reaction: -identify what is the worst part of this situation

*Remember – <u>do not</u> go around the circle for this or subsequent phases

Symptoms: -identify the cognitive, physical, emotional, behavioral and spiritual signs of distress being experienced by the participants

"How is life different for you since the event?"

Teaching: -normalize the symptoms

-discuss coping strategies (psychological)

-discuss stress management strategies (physiological)

-discuss resources available

-instill hope

Re-entry: -summarize themes

-discuss any new issues/concerns brought forward

-offer individual follow-up immediately after the group is over

The Critical Incident Stress Debriefing is a vehicle to mitigating the impact of the crisis event and facilitating the restoration of functioning. In addition, participation in a CISD allows for the identification of those individuals who need additional support.

The 5-step modified CISD is utilized under 3 conditions: line of duty death, suicide or participants are 6-12 years old. The modifications are the same:

In the cases of line of duty death and suicide, the 5-step debriefing is general done on the day of the event in place of a defusing. It is modified to a 5-step process because of the intense emotions involved in these situations.

The rationale for modifying the CISD process when dealing with students who are 6-12 years of age is a little different. Essentially shortening the process is a response to shorter attention spans, limited language skills and a tendency towards concrete or "magical" thinking. In addition, the younger the student, the more suggestible they are thus care must be taken when normalizing reactions.

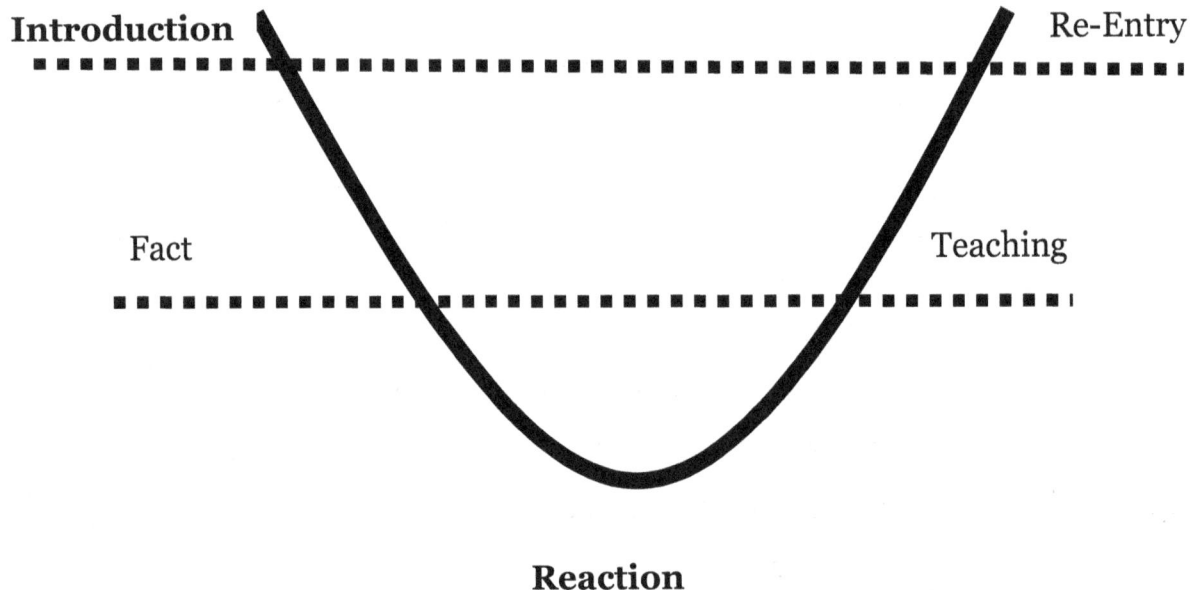

Introduction   Re-Entry

Fact   Teaching

Reaction

Exercise: Critical Incident Stress Debriefing

Describe 3 observations made in each phase:

Introduction:

Fact:

Thought:

Reaction:

Symptoms:

Teaching:

Re-entry:

Were the transitions between phases smooth or natural?

Were the phases followed in order?

Were the questions stated clearly?

Was there any evidence of probing? Describe

Comments:

Intervention Comparison Chart

Intervention	Target	Timing	Duration	Team
CMB	Heterogeneous groups	Any time new information is available	20-30 minutes	Administrator and member of crisis team
Defusing	Homogenous groups	Up to 8–12 hours post incident	20-45 minutes	2+ trained members of crisis team
CISD	Homogenous group	1-10 days post event	1-3 hours	2+ trained members of crisis team ; 1 must be a MHP
Individual	Single person	Any time	15-20 minutes	1 trained member of crisis team

Note: Use of these intervention techniques are not mutually exclusive. Rather, using the right technique at the right time with well-trained individuals leads to the best outcome.

SECTION FIVE
SUICIDE PREVENTION AND INTERVENTION

According to the Center for Disease Control and Prevention (CDC-2015), suicide is the 3rd leading cause of death among persons ages 10-14 and the second among persons aged 15-34. Approximately 4,600 youth commit suicide each year. In addition, they report that among students in grades 9-12 in the U.S. during 2013: 17% of students seriously considered attempting suicide in the previous 12 months (22.4% of females and 11.6% of males).

Providing crisis intervention services in a school setting following a completed suicide is one of the most challenging situations that any administrator can face. The highly charged emotions of the student's peers and faculty reactions are complicated by the various values and beliefs attracted to the act itself. The location, mechanism of death (bullet wound, strangulation, etc.) and timing of death all can influence efforts to stabilize the situation. Parent and family needs and wishes add to the stresses of dealing with the fallout of a completed suicide... Social media also plays a strong role in how a suicide is understood and managed.

In an attempt to assist schools and communities in dealing with the public health crisis of youth suicide, the United States Congress passed the Garrett Lee Smith Memorial Act in 2004. This Act was signed in to law by President George W. Bush with the intention of providing states with the funds to develop comprehensive suicide prevention and early intervention strategies specifically for youth. This Act was followed by the adoption of the Jason Flatt Act by over 27 states. The Jason Flatt Act specifically requires that all public, charter, technical/trade schools and tribal educators receive specific training in recognition of warning signs and early intervention strategies.

Warning signs – things youth do or say when they are contemplating suicide:

- talking about wanting to die or to kill oneself

- talking about feeling trapped or unbearable pain

- talk about feeling hopeless and/or helpless

- talk about being a burden to others

- sudden changes in behavior

- increased use of drugs or alcohol

- withdrawal or self-isolation

- showing rage or talking about seeking revenge

- loss of interest in things one cares about

- decline in school performance

- behaving recklessly

- saying goodbye to family and friends

- giving possessions away

Risk Factors – characteristics or conditions that increase the chance that a person may attempt suicide:

- history of or current mental health disorders (e.g. depression, bi-polar, anxiety)

- alcohol or drug abuse

- previous suicide attempts

- family history of suicide attempts or completed suicides

- LGBT identity or feelings

- situational stressors (e.g. parental separation or divorce, loss of a relationship, pregnancy, change of school)

- history of abuse or exposure to family/community violence

- poor impulse control or hyperactivity

- access to a gun

School administrators are required to provide for the "care, welfare and safety" of all students. Therefore, specific policies and procedures for how to deal with a potentially suicidal student should be developed, distributed and reviewed with faculty members and support staff. These policies and procedures should take into consideration all local and state laws as well as local resources.

Things to be considered when dealing with a potentially suicidal student are:

1. Maintaining a calm and safe environment for the student

2. Who can conduct the suicide screening/assessment

3. When/whom/how to inform parent or guardian; advise of safety measures to be taken at home

4. Accessing a clinical evaluation; referral resources for treatment

5. Safety planning

Suicide Contagion

"Suicide contagion refers to the process whereby one suicide or suicidal act within a school, community or geographic area increases the likelihood that others will attempt or die by suicide." - National Youth Mental Health Foundation 2015.

It is tragic enough to have the death of one student or faculty member be the result of a completed suicide; it is catastrophic to have more than one or even multiple deaths occur. Though suicide "clusters" are rare, they tend to be most prevalent among adolescents. Research now suggests that all suicides are preventable with adequate training and vigilance. However, there are those individuals that are more vulnerable to suicidal thoughts following a completed suicide than others.

These include:

- those that are closest (physically and relationally) to the person who completed suicide

Barbara J. Ertl, MS, LPC, NCC & Dr. Mary Schoenfeldt

- those that witness a completed suicide

- those that are socially marginalized

- those that had previously attempted suicide

- those with a prior history of trauma

When a suicide occurs that impacts a school setting, exceptional vigilance and effort must be given to the students and staff that fall in to these categories. When a crisis team member encounters a person who may be contemplating a suicide attempt, it may be helpful to utilize the SAFER-R protocol that has been modified to address suicidal ideation

It is as follows:

Stabilization: plus introduction

Acknowledge: the event and reactions

> **- clarify:** "Do you really want to die, or do you want to change the way you are living your life."

Facilitation: of understanding = normalization

> **- contradict via:**

>> ---desired outcome will not be achieved

>> ---suicide will create more problems than it will solve

>> ---suicide creates an adverse and undesired "ripple effect" affecting others

Encourage: effective coping

> **- delay**

Refer for continued care

ALWAYS ASSIST IN ACCESSING A HIGHER LEVEL OF CARE!

SECTION SIX
LESSONS LEARNED

National Applications

- **Sandy Hook Elementary School Shooting**

- **The Townville Elementary School Shooting**

International Applications

- **The Australian Experience**

- **Psychological First Aid Internationally... Using Charades**

Sandy Hook

Lessons in Public Communications & Community Relations
Following a Crisis

By Dr. Mary Schoenfeldt

I volunteered for 10 days at Newton, Connecticut, arrive ng a few weeks after the December 2012 Sandy Hook shooting incident. I was invited because of my in-depth experience with school safety and emergency preparedness. From an emergency management and communications perspective, my initial observations included:

- This was not a school shooting (the school itself was not "targeted"); it was a shooting at a school (could have occurred anywhere there were young children).

- Though the town had significant resources, there were layers of impact: emergency managers, city departments, communications, school system, and the community...the emotional toll was very high (everyone knew someone who died).

  ✓ Throngs of media and visitors (including President Obama, Anderson Cooper and Dr. Phil) overwhelmed the downtown area – significant gridlock and economic impacts and the population essentially doubled for a period of weeks.

  ✓ 21 funerals were held within a one-week period; Post Office inundated with millions of sympathy cards.

  ✓ 60,000 teddy bears were donated and had to be stored /distributed/disposed of.

  ✓ $7.5 million donated to families within four weeks created distribution and tax implication issues.

- Communications is often chaotic – even on a good day, initially, law enforcement was the lead agency, but there was little continuation of a Joint Information Center/Joint Information System after they stood down". Belief is when law enforcement is done, the "job is done". But that's not the case. The community still has work to do.

Lessons learned...

- *Nurture city leadership groups* and know who to contact. Examples: **1)** Organized clergy and association of funeral directors managed high volume and coordination of burials; **2)** Rotary helped provide humanitarian services; **3)** Post Office, Youth and Family Services, Adventists, and other organizations managed volunteer coordination.

- *Prepare for unrequested donations.* Pro-active public directives telling people how they can best help will mitigate this.

- *Establish a communications hub.* Plan for one in your area before disaster strikes. Example: Centrally located, but out of the impact zo ne, Newton's Blue Colony Diner became the place to go for learning know was going on and when public meetings were scheduled.

- *Plan for memorials* – spontaneous and intentional –and develop a policy in advance.

- *Anticipate small business impacts* – apply for economic relief after a disaster.

- *Schools should have their family reunifications plan in place*, drills conducted, and a roster of retired professionals to draw upon for support and to backfill positions. This helps create comfort and stability for students and faculty once school is resumed.

- *Share "feel good" stories with the media* during the recovery. Example: The school moved to a new building that featured fully replicated classrooms (down to the items that were on the students' desk when they evacuated), making the transition to "normalcy" easier

- *Be strategic in timing for notifying families of victims.* Example: Circle of support groups (a chaplain, state trooper, and mental health professional) notified all families at the exact same time and escorted them to a private area to pick up victims' belongings.

- *Anticipate simultaneous media interview needs.* Produce multiple "common brand" backdrops/posters for different spokespersons to stand in front during press conferences.

- *Responding to a tragic event impacts you too* - it's difficult to remain objective. Your judgement may be impaired. The longer you are on shift, the more likely you think you can do more/work a longer shift.

- ***No system/agency is "alone" – use your resources*** (i.e. Admin staff and volunteers; neighboring jurisdictions; local, state and regional EC/JIC). Ask for help even if you don't think you'll need it – it's easier to "stand down" than it is to activate 48 hours into an incident.

- ***PIO/Communications job during a major crisis is usually different than day-to-day responsibilities.*** Plan for it and develop pre-canned messages and press releases now; then just fill in the blanks for a given incident.

Newton Connecticut did a great job of coordinating and managing the unthinkable. As in any incident of this scope, there was chaos and confusion. But they kept those at a minimum considering the monumental challenges they faced. We all can learn from their experience...from what they did right and what they wish they might have done differently.

In a situation such as this, the whole community will be challenged and will be changed forever. "Business as usual" will be impossible so now is the time to think about it, prepare for it, and plan for it.

The Townville Elementary School Shooting

By Tina S. Brookes, EdD. MSW, LCSW

Prior to the Sept. 28, 2016 shooting at Townville Elementary School, I had established trust and credibility with the local emergency responders through CISM training and consultation regarding team building. Therefore, after the school shooting I was requested to provide CISD services to the two 911 call centers who were actively involved in the incident since Townville Elementary School was located on a county line. Following the CISD a local chaplain asked for my recommendations about how to bring the students back to school after the funeral of six-year-old Jacob Hall.

I shared with the Chaplain the lessons learned I had gained from a prior visit with the Student Services Director, Betsy Thompson, of Jefferson County Public Schools where Columbine High School is located. I suggested it was best if the students could return to school during an "Open House". This allows parents and family members to attend with their students, which provides extra support and supervision for the students. It also allows students the opportunity to walk their parents and family members through the school and show them where they were located during the shooting, the evacuation path they took, and where the shooting took place. Doing this walk-through during an "Open House" gives everyone; faculty, staff, students, and families, as much time as needed to linger and discuss any questions. It gives an opportunity for folks to return to school at their own pace. It is my understanding most of the student body took advantage of the "Open House" and it was very well received.

The following day the school was opened with the goal for it to be as 'regular' a school day as possible. Of course this goal was relative. There were extensive support staff available and many parents accompanied their students to class as would be expected following a critical incident.

I was invited to provide CISM support to the two First Grade classes that directly experienced the shooting. All of the live-fire was directed at one classroom where Jacob Hall was tragically shot and later died. Two other students and a teacher were also shot and wounded. The other class of students was out on the playground and witnessed the entire incident.

I was first asked to support the classroom that witnessed the shooting from the playground. I had a Classroom Discussion that is a school-modified version of the Crisis Management Briefing. I introduced my team and myself: 3 adults; one young adult and, a HOPE-Animal Assisted Crisis Response Team. NOTE: All of my team members were trained in CISM and working with children and schools in crisis.

Next, I allowed students to pet our large HOPE St. Bernard in designated groups of four while my young adult counted slowly to 10. At that time we changed the groups so another group of four could pet the dog. The HOPE team was located in the back of the classroom and only those children who requested it went back to pet the dog.

Then, I asked the students to describe what they saw during the school shooting. Many of the students remembered clearly details from that afternoon. As one student talked others would agree or disagree until everyone was satisfied I had been given the facts accurately.

Next, I did some education. I explained about the Human Stress Response on a developmentally appropriate level; "Of course you ran. That is one of the things the body tells you to do when you see something so frightening. Some of you may have been frozen in place and could not run. That happens too." I also normalized the Post Traumatic Stress symptoms they had discussed. The children were hungry to hear the education piece. They did not cry. We all talked about the details in a very matter of fact and calm manner.

I finished by discussing with the children how sad Jacob's family must be by his death and I suggested they create cards for the family so they will know how much the students cared. The students were happy to do that and the entire team monitored the room during this activity. Later in the day the students also made cards for the teacher and 2 students who were shot and injured.

I then took my team to the other classroom and repeated the Classroom Discussion and Education format.

Lessons Learned: The classroom of students who witnessed the shooting had vivid and detailed memories. They experienced PTS and wanted to know what had happened to them. They were a significant group to target for intervention. However, many if not most of the responders to the school were focused on the classroom where Jacob was shot. It seemed everyone wanted to talk to these students as "Ground Zero". I believe there is sufficient evidence to suggest that the onlookers absorbed a tremendous amount of sensory input and were just as important a "Ground Zero" target.

It was also obvious that not all students like dogs. Many have allergies to them. My two HOPE-Animal Assisted Crisis Response Teams handlers are well trained in CISM and they were careful to read body language of the students and respond appropriately. They also watched their dogs and knew when to give the animals a break from the students. Unfortunately, we all witnessed some other dog teams in the building whose handlers were not as well trained. I totally support having dogs available for students following a school crisis, however, the dog and the adult handlers must be well-trained in crisis response.

The Australian Experience

By Monica Kleinman

INTRODUCTION

After being trained in CISM in the Australian Army where I served as a Reservist Psychology Officer for some 27 years, I was readily able to see how the program could be adapted and modified for application in schools from kindergarten to year 12 final year in my state.

With a similarly minded colleague we wrote a package subsequently implemented across the state and in other states also. The program needed, of course, to take into consideration a significant number of unique factors ranging from the fact that we were applying psychological services to minors hence requiring parental consent to the very different nature of school cultures across the very different locations from inner city to very remote.

What assisted in this was the fact that all schools had access to school psychologists in the public sector, the one the program was targeting, and these psychologists were able to move across school districts and regions as deemed appropriate to provide interventions after crises. The program was run out in around 1992.

UPTAKE

All public schools were required to prepare CISM policy documents and the program we developed dovetailed very well with that mandated obligation as it enabled schools to insert school, location, developmental age and other dynamic aspects into both their policy document and the program as it was introduced to their particular school communities.

INCIDENTS

Almost immediately the program was applied to a range of crises. Amongst those that stand out are the following de-identified events.

1. A man enters a family home where his ex-girlfriend lives and shoots her dead as well as another person living in that house. He then drives to another suburb and shoots dead another individual. The first victim was a teacher at one school, the third was a parent of children at another school. The first victim's new partner was a police officer attached to the station sent out to investigate the first shootings and he attended this location as a first responder. Both he and his fiancé were well known in that community as was the second victim and the third in that separate community. Provision was made with the local school to provide services that now, looking back with a better understanding of best practice, were clearly well within the psychological first aid guidelines.

Barbara J. Ertl, MS, LPC, NCC & Dr. Mary Schoenfeldt

Breakout classrooms were identified for the teacher's current class, and for her classes taught in previous years. The school staff was relieved of their teaching duties for that day to allow them to choose how they wished either to be supported themselves of to support their students. After the end of that school day, a community gathering was organized where school, community, police and other first responders could meet. An interview with local TV alerted parents to possible impact on their children especially as there was extensive and on-going police action with sirens till very late at night. Staff and students were monitored. No group interventions were implemented on this occasion. Sub judice concerns precluded this.

2. A group of around five 15-16 yr. olds ride their bikes up a particularly steep mountain with the purpose of racing downhill. All are from the same year at the same school. One lad is seen by the others to disable his brakes, subsequently rides off the edge of the mountain and is killed. His parents refuse to accept there was any intent and do not permit any mention of the 'suicide' word.

A whole school assembly is held to advise the school of the death of the student. The other four boys did not attend school for some days. The funeral was conducted a few days later once the body had been released by the coroner and the whole school once again met for a brief memorial recognition. The cohort of students, year 9, was offered support as were any others that self-identified but the 'suicide' word was not to be used making all interventions somewhat artificial as the disabling of the bike brakes was very quickly known to most.

3. A teacher at a primary school, (ages 5-12) was removed from his duties as allegations of improper conduct were investigated. It is my belief that events like this have the potential to expand exponentially as alignments are formed for or against, as individuals with their own agendas or histories decompensate and experience potentially serious consequences and, once again, the legal process takes precedence so group interventions are not realistic.

In this instance, support was provided to the principal and his management team on how best to address the multiple concerns including, of course, from the parent body but also from previous school communities where this teacher had worked.

4. On a school excursion, a year 7 (first yr. of high school) student dies after an asthma attack. While her asthma was known, there was nothing to indicate the severity of the condition and she had been reportedly using her medications in compliance with instructions. She was found deceased in her remote camping location where the yr. 7 cohort were undergoing a program with trained Yr. 11 (age 16-17) students acting as mentors supervised by teachers and teachers' aides.

The first priority was to return the whole group to their home locations, a not insignificant enterprise as buses not pre-arranged had to be located, parents had to be informed and school policies and procedures were examined almost immediately even if only from Department of Education senior officials. Group interventions were provided for the students who had shared her bunk house and were offered to others who asked for support but timing was problematic given the students were dispatched to their parents'

58

care and many did not immediately return to school. While the student who had died was known to others from her primary school, this exercise was undertaken well before the entire cohort of new Yr. 7 students knew each other.

Barbara J. Ertl, MS, LPC, NCC & Dr. Mary Schoenfeldt

Psychological First Aid Internationally... Using Charades

By Nathan Ray, MSW

"We want you to teach the principles of psychological first aid (PFA) and Critical Incident Stress Management (CISM) to a group of teenagers. It needs to be done in about half the time you would normally spend during a training session. None of the teens speak English, so you will be using interpreters. And it will take place in a foreign country so the Americanized examples you usually use won't work".

This was the challenge presented for our Rotary and Green Cross Academy of Traumatology service trip to Leogane and Merger, Haiti, in early 2014, four years after the devastating earthquake that caused so much damage to that country. Our group of eight team members planned to adapt and teach disaster preparation, response, and recovery to the community that had been at the epicenter of the earthquake. We were asked to teach the teens because they were the future village leaders, would be able to attend a week-long course and could share their learning with the adults, along with the younger children in the community.

The first stage was paring down the wealth of information and ideas from a typical PFA or CISM training presented in the USA into something usable in the circumstances described above. After several times through the materials used in trainings for disaster response classes, the following concepts were chosen as the core learning: What makes an event traumatic; types of trauma; typical responses to trauma; Comparison of PFA to medical first aid; Goals of PFA; Principles of PFA; and Self-care techniques. This material was condensed into about 25 simple PowerPoint slides. Because there was no guarantee electricity would be available at the training site, care was taken to ensure the slides would be usable in a printed version as well.

Stage two involved further editing and adapting of the material and presentation to reach our expected audience. A translation program was used so the concepts on each slide were presented in English and Haitian Creole. Research was done to provide examples of traumatic events typical to Haiti, rather than the USA. Pictorial examples were replaced with images from Haiti. The presentation was practiced with someone repeating the words in English, then giving responses twice in an effort to approximate the timing needed for interpretation, which resulted in editing the length from about 25 down to 15 multilingual slides.

Final preparation was conducted in the days leading up to the presentation. Similar adaptation had been done to the "practical" skills of disaster response – medical first aid, triage, building extrication, etc. – and these were taught to the group of teenagers over the first 3 days of our week-long training. Our training team met each evening and discussed how the day had gone. We highlighted what seemed to have worked, what could have gone better, and how our students were processing the materials. Two themes emerged from these discussions: 1) our students thrived on interactive material and 2) they became much more engaged when concepts were tied to their own lives and what they already knew.

60

On the evening of day 3, the presentation was revamped again. Pictures of our students engaged in training were inserted into the slides, replacing many of the more generic Haitian pictures that had already taken the place of our American examples. Several interactive games and exercises were discussed and even tried by the instructors before deciding that adding charades would be the best way to engage our students. About 12 hours before the PFA training was scheduled to begin, the presentation took its final form.

The typical audience for disaster training in the USA contains of a mix of professional first responders, para-professionals who have some training already, and citizen volunteers who are interested in learning more about being prepared and helping their community. Almost all are adults with a wide range of experiences and education. They are not 13- to 18-year olds still in middle and high school who have already survived their homes being destroyed and watched family and friends die or be injured. They do not carry scars and disfigurement from their own disaster experiences. But this was our audience that day.

We started the day in typical fashion, thanking the students for their time and participation; then reviewing skills and concepts taught in previous sessions. After a few minutes of this, we moved into discussing what thoughts and emotions had been brought up while going through the training. Talking through interpreters sometimes made discussion cumbersome, but it also added to the depth of conversation because the interpreters often asked clarifying questions to ensure meaning and they added their own thoughts to those of both instructors and audience. Identifying that the training had reminded many of the students of their experiences in the earthquake (and in other, smaller, traumatic events) provided an excellent transition into the day's coursework.

Students, interpreters, and community leaders who were also attending the training quickly recognized the importance of addressing the psychological impact of trauma and provided examples from their own lives. This was not a theoretical exercise for them, but a very real and personal issue. When the discussion moved to intentional interventions, it was time for charades. Several older teens of both genders volunteered for a "fishbowl" exercise. One volunteer was given the role of having received bad news about a family member and two others were tasked with practicing PFA. They really got into their roles and the audience cheered them on with encouragement and ideas. Our female PFA practitioner gave the victim a hug, while the male PFA practitioner sat next to the victim and rested a hand on his shoulder while talking with him. A few other volunteer groups practiced similar scenarios after that and, without exception, the PFA practitioners made sure to include an appropriate hug in their intervention.

That evening, while debriefing on the day, the instructor group noted that this was the first time in our experiences where the students had been so involved. The day was full of laughter and excitement that went beyond typical PFA or CISM instruction and it was because the students were so engaged. The following day consisted of tying all the lessons together, planning for the future, and graduation exercises. Throughout the day, instructors noticed students hugging and supporting each other more than they had earlier in the week. Although the teaching had been edited down severely from a "standard" PFA training, it seemed that being flexible in our teaching approach and style paid off and the students really took it to heart.

When teaching in an international setting, the key is to be flexible and willing to try something outside of the norm. There will be obstacles including language and culture, but those can become part of the learning experience for both instructors and students.

REFERENCES

American Academy of Pediatrics; www.aap.org.

Brock, Stephen E.; Reeves, Melissa; Jimerson, Shane R.; Lieberman, Richard; Nickerson, Amanda; Feinberg, Theodore. (2009) *School Crisis Prevention and Intervention: The PrePare Model.* NASP Publishing.

Center for Disease Control and Prevention: Resources for schools after traumatic incidents

Center for Disease Control and Prevention: About the CDC-Kaiser ACE Study http://wwww.cdc.gove/violenceprevention/acestudy/about.html Accessed July 10, 2017

Center for Disease Control and Prevention: Suicide Facts at a Glance. 2015 https:/Ac/www.cdc.gov/violenceprevention/pdf/suicide-datasheet-a.pdf Accessed August 8, 2017

Dube, Shanta R., Anda, Robert F., Felitti, Vincent J., et al. (2001) Childhood Abuse, Household Dysfunction, and the Risk of Attempted Suicide Throughout the Life Span: Findings From the Adverse Childhood Experience Study. *Journal of the American Medical Assn.* 286 (24), 3089-3096.

Everly, G.S., Jr. (1995) *Crisis Intervention: The SAFER-R Model. Innovations in Disaster and Trauma Psychology.* Vol 1, 194-206. Ellicott City, MD: Chevron Publishing.

Everly, G.S., Jr., Mitchell, J.T. (2013). *Critical Incident Stress Management (CISM): Key Papers and Core Concepts.* Ellicott City, MD. Chevron Publishing.

Felitti, Vincent J. et al (1998). Relationship of Childhood Abuse and Household Dysfunction to Many of the Leading Causes of Death in Adults. *American Journal of Preventative Medicine* 14(4), 245-258.

FEMA; Guide for Developing High-Quality School Emergency Operations Plan

Garrett Lee Smith Act of 2004; reauthorized in 2015

Goldstein, D.B., Walrath, C.M., McKeon, R., Puddy, R.W., Lubell, K.M., Potter, L.B., & Roch, M.S. (2010). The Garrett Lee Smith Memorial Suicide Prevention Program. *Suicide & Life – Threatening Behavior*, 40(3), 245-256.

Jason Flatt Act of 2007

Mitchell, J.T. (2007). Group Crisis Support: Why It Works, When and How to Provide It. Ellicott City, MD. Chevron Publishing.

Mitchell, J.T. (2006). *Strategic Response to Crisis*. Ellicott City, MD. The International Critical Incident Stress Foundation.

National Child Traumatic Stress Network; www.nctsn.org.

Nelson, D.E., Powell-Griner, E., Town, M., Kovar, M.G. (2003) A Comparison of National Estimates From the National Health Interview Survey and the Behavioral Role Factor Surveillance System. *American Journal of Public Health* 93: 1335-1341.

REMS; (Readiness in Emergency Management) for Schools; www.rems.ed.gov.

Sacks, Vanessa; Murphy, David; Moore, Kristin. (2014) Adverse Childhood Experiences: National and State-Level Prevalence. *Child Trends*, 2014-28.

Yalom, I.D. (2005). *The Theory and Practice of Group Psychology*. New York, NY. Basic Books.

APPENDIX I
EXCERPT FROM PICKING UP THE PIECES:
Responding To School Crisis by Dr. Mary Schoenfeldt

NOTE: The term Incident Management Team is used interchangeable at times in this except with the term Critical Incident Stress Management Team. In many districts, the CISM team is a sub team of a broader Incident Management Team.

Chapter 1
Crisis in the Schools: General Information

The phone in your office rings just before school starts for the day. Your secretary is informed that two of your students have been involved in a serious accident as they were walking to school. What do you do now? Who do you call? What effect will this have on your other students? What about staff?

What you do **does** make a difference, and the first 48 hours are the most critical. As in any traumatic situation, it is during those hours that human beings attempt to make sense of what has happened. Ideally, the goal of any Incident Management Team is to return to the pre-trauma, "normal" state as soon as possible. Delaying intervention increases the chance of long-term emotional distress and possibly Post-Traumatic Stress Syndrome.

We know that crisis as well as school violence, and the trauma resulting from it, is increasing dramatically. Combined with the surge of violence in society in general, it creates fertile ground for both students and adults to have difficulty coping with everyday life. For students, this translates into difficulty learning as well as other problems.

Additional to violence, the incidents of accidental death or injury have skyrocketed with the increased use of alcohol and other drugs (AODs) among young people. One young high school woman reported losing 11 friends to AOD-related incidents during her sophomore year. We know for certain these increasing experiences are having an effect on a student's mental and emotional health.

Until recently, schools have had to deal with only an occasional traumatic event or crisis. Now, however, they are increasingly being caught off guard and left saying, "I never dreamed that could happen here. Thank goodness it is over and now we can return to normal." What many of these schools fail to realize is that "normal" will never be the same again. Until now, each school administrator had taken what he or she believed was the best course of action for the staff and students. That course of action often varied greatly from site to site. We now know that some actions are helpful while others, though well intended, increase trauma. Removing the belongings from the classroom of a student who has died, for example, may further traumatize his/her classmates if not done respectfully and appropriately.

Some of the questions we ask ourselves aren't easy to answer. Should we allow students to go to the funeral service? How flexible should we encourage teachers to be in their classrooms following an event? What kind of support does the staff need to more effectively meet the needs of kids? We now have the answers to these questions and others, and do not have to guess any more. We know what to look for in the months following that might indicate unhealthy coping mechanisms even though there may be no visible signs.

We know that people who have been affected by trauma need places to acknowledge what has happened and to receive support from others. Allowing students and staff to attend funeral or memorial services in some circumstances may provide a sense of closure and allow healing to begin. Within the classroom, teachers need to provide the opportunity for students to express themselves while still maintaining a structure that is as close to normal as possible. Staff also needs places to express their feelings of grief and loss so that they can be emotionally available to provide support to students and parents.

Schools need to have a proactive plan in place to deal with a crisis **before** it happens rather than simply reacting and hoping for the best. A complete plan includes an emergency management plan, a district-level Incident Management Team and a site-level Incident Management Team to take the leadership role and make decisions concerning the needs of students and staff.

The site-level Incident Management Team should work in conjunction with the student assistance program, if one is in place, and in fact, might include some of the same people. Team members should reflect all levels of the school, from administrators, teaching staff and classified staff to parents and students. A CISM Team would be an invaluable resource.

They would be responsible for coordinating resources, planning and running staff information and debriefing meetings and centralizing communication between parents, staff, students, district personnel, media and the community. They would also be available to assist individual teachers with classroom notification of the incident, provide a "safe" room for both students and staff to come if they need extra support, coordinate all paperwork and record keeping, and refer individuals to community resources, the student assistance program, employee assistance program, etc.

The CISM team creates a specific plan of action for the day, the next week, month and six months. That plan includes an evaluation component of what worked and what needs to be adjusted. This team may also coordinates appropriate staff training in areas such as suicide prevention, the grieving process, critical incident stress management, etc. The primary goal of this team is to support staff who in turn can support students.

Schools that have Incident Management Teams are better able to respond immediately to a crisis by implementing a plan already in place. They have a list of key personnel, their day and evening phone numbers and their responsibilities and functions. Ideally, this list is three to five people deep in the event that someone on the list can't be reached or is a victim of the crisis. Valuable time is not wasted in making decisions during the crisis about who to call, where to reach them and what to do now.

With a plan in place the team can immediately be mobilized to begin the process of confirming the information and coordinating the systematic response needed to support both students and staff to return to a pre-trauma state of "normal" as soon as possible. The response is consistent and based on current research and information of how to best cope with the particular situation. By having a team in place, with an up-to-date action plan (this book can be a guide), administrators eliminate the guesswork that would result from hearing the news of a crisis and saying, "Oh no! I never thought that would happen here. What do we do now?"

Barbara J. Ertl, MS, LPC, NCC & Dr. Mary Schoenfeldt

School Bus Accident

Overview: Nature of Event

A school bus accident is a very impactful event for everyone. The risk of multiple injuries is high. The reaction to any injury or loss of life can be extremely wrenching. Students and parents alike may be angry and question whether it is safe to ride on your buses. Schools may have to provide information on the safety records of the drivers, maintenance records of the buses and descriptions of safety programs presented to children to help calm parent's fears. The accident investigation may go on for a long period of time and the issue of fault and legal liability will certainly be explored. The first 24 hours will be critical to set the tone of the incident in the public's mind. Be open to questions but don't speculate or give opinions until the investigation has been completed.

Plan:

- Confirm information of accident

- Convene Incident Management Team

- Notify appropriate district level personnel, including Risk Manager

- Arrange for transportation to school of uninjured students and adults

- Notify parents of students involved in the accident

- Set up a receiving center for those students coming to school who were on the bus but not injured

- Assign at least 2 adults to the receiving center to welcome kids to school and allow them to defuse before they go to their classrooms

- When uninjured students go to their classroom, have an adult accompany them to help deflect attention and questions

- Identify which students and adults were on that specific bus

- Deploy Incident Management Team members to each hospital that is receiving injured students or adults to act as liaisons

- Contact translators to assist at school and at the hospitals if appropriate

68

- Begin notifying parents or guardians of injured children to go to the appropriate hospital

- Access emergency medical information on injured and relay to hospital

- Contact feeder schools with information

- Write a statement for the media assuring the majority of parents that their children are safe

- Write a statement or fact sheet to be used by the people answering telephones in the school office

- Write a statement to be read by Incident Management Team members in each classroom

- Assist classroom teachers to allow students to talk about the event

- Begin activating additional support resources

- Set up Safe Rooms

- Document all actions taken

Continuing Response:

- Incident Management Team does a Tactical Debriefing Meeting to discuss next steps

- Prepare for parents wanting to pick their children up from school at the end of the day

- Assign Incident Management Team members to be visible and direct traffic after school

- Update information of injured students and adults

- Meet with families to give information. Have translators available if needed

- Mobilize counseling resources from neighboring school sites or the community

- Contact parent volunteer or prearranged local business to get juice, cookies, Kleenex and other supplies for the Safe Rooms

- Arrange for a trained staff member or community mental health professional to be available by phone to answer parents' questions or concerns

- Discuss anticipated reactions

- Contact police to cooperate in the ongoing accident investigation

- Identify high-risk students or staff

- PIO (Public Information Officer) prepare statement for media

- Have family liaison contact victims' families to support

Overview: Special Considerations

Any incident that involves injury or death to young people is particularly traumatic for a school community. The first priority is to communicate with all those involved or affected. The Incident Management Team needs to activate a command post at the school or district office so it has access to emergency plans, medical records, phone numbers, etc. If the bus accident happens in another community (while the debate team is at an "away" event, for instance), it is advisable to send at least one Incident Management Team member to the location of the accident to coordinate and relay information.

An information center should be set up in the gym or a multipurpose room to give parents, staff and community members a central location for information and support. Post signs directing people to the info center and have beverages and cookies available as well as a bulletin board or other mechanism to update information as it becomes available from the command post. Activate community assistance to provide support. Counselors from other school districts, community chaplains or other clergy, or community mental health counselors are good resources to be available to talk with people as they wait for information. Make sure the counseling resources sign in at the command post with the community liaison of the school Incident Management Team. Arrange for supervision of children that may come with parents and have games, drawing materials, stuffed animals, movies, or other activities available to keep children occupied.

If the accident happens before or during school, you may be able to handle the incident within your normal daily structure. Handle this like any other traumatic incident that happens during school hours. Write a script to be used for classroom notification. Encourage students and staff to talk about their reactions, set up Safe Rooms. Cancel activities like history tests; assess students who seem particularly vulnerable. Contact parents of extremely upset students. Keep the media away from students, staff and parents and plan for the rest of your response. You may want to open your gym or multipurpose room as an information center. It's important for people to be together to receive information and begin to put words to the emotion that the event has caused. Even though it is chaotic, there isn't a need to close school early or do an early dismissal procedure. There is no danger at school and the very structure of being on the school campus until regular dismissal time is comforting in its familiarity. By keeping your normal dismissal time, it also gives those students who drive their own vehicles time to react before they get behind the wheel of their cars.

If it happens after school or on a weekend, the specific activities to respond would need to be altered to include an Incident Management Team meeting (at least by phone) to plan for expected reactions and activities, opening school for an information center, contacting the District PIO (Public Information Officer) to set up a press conference, sending a team member to the location of the accident to relay information and act as school district contact.

Media relations will be crucial. Be aware that the first 24 hours will frame the public's perception of the incident. If you are defensive, evasive or uncooperative, it won't matter what you do or say after that time; the reputation and credibility will be damaged. Also be very cautious not to speculate prematurely on the cause.

Depending on the situation, reporters may be at the hospital, the accident scene and your school, looking to interview students, staff and parents. If it is a very serious accident, you might get a flood of media from all over the country. (They will tend to be the most aggressive because they have nothing to lose and everything to gain.) The local police department may have its spokesperson at the accident scene to handle reporters there. The district should also have a representative there to assist them.

At your schools and the hospital, use site- and district-level public information representatives to communicate with the media. Prepare statements and update them frequently. Making an appearance every 15 minutes or so to say, "We have no new information at this time, but as soon as we do we will let you know," will do much to keep reporters informed and controlled.

When working with the media, keep a few things in mind. Do not give out any names. Do not allow the media access to the distraught friends, families or other students. Also, if you need assistance, your local law enforcement agency may be able to help you set up and maintain media areas.

Whatever is said in the first 24 hours will create the general impression and theme of the incident. Be very cautious not to prematurely speculate on cause.

You may have to decide whether to cancel a scheduled event like a school play. In most instances, it is best to keep as normal a structure as you can. You might give the option of canceling to the students involved themselves. Ask the student actors and stage crew, for instance, if they need to cancel the performance or do they feel like they want to go ahead and just dedicate the performance or observe a moment of silence before it begins. After a tragedy, it's important to maintain as much "normalcy" as possible and that includes continuing with planned events if there is no danger or damage that is done by holding the event.

Key Resources

You will need resources for several functions. One will be to provide Critical Incident Stress Management activities to your school community. Another is to provide relief for staff that might have difficulty dealing with the event.

If the event is a very traumatic one, using "outsiders" as crisis counselors may be the best course of action. When we become "secondary" victims, we lose our objectivity and need support ourselves. Bringing knowledgeable, sensitive people into your classrooms allows students, faculty and staff not only to get answers to their questions but also to address their fears. The key is that anyone providing counseling should be trained in handling adolescents and school systems. They also need to check in with the community liaison on the Incident Management Team and document their attendance and activities.

A Parent Informational Evening will be necessary to restore the parents' beliefs that their children are safe. Local law enforcement and mental health professionals should play a large role in that meeting. A representative of the district's transportation department or the company handling the district's bus service should be at that meeting to answer questions and to provide reassurance.

Resources to deal with a traumatic event can come from a variety of places. At the local level, many communities have agencies (such as a county mental health department) and private organizations that do crisis counseling. Some police and fire agencies have trained staff that may help with Critical Incident Stress Management. Arranging with neighboring schools to mobilize their counseling staff in the event of a crisis is another way to have extra resources available.

Beyond the local level, most states have networks of Critical Incident Stress Management teams who can be mobilized quickly to come and assist. And the International Critical Incident Stress Foundation maintains a list of Critical Incident Stress Management teams throughout the world.

Safe Rooms Considerations

A <u>Student Safe Room</u> is a designated place where students can go if they are having difficulty maintaining their composure in a regular supportive classroom environment. It should be staffed by at least two people and be equipped with tissues, drawing and writing materials, stuffed animals, appropriate literature and refreshments such as cookies and juice.

An attendance procedure needs to be in place to manage the tendency of students to leave classrooms and then just wander around campus. It is recommended that students sign out of their regular classroom and then sign in to the Safe Room within a certain time limit. If a student is having a particularly difficult time dealing with the loss, it may be advisable to contact his or her parents or guardian and to notify a counselor. Discourage students from leaving in their own cars if they are upset. Contact parents to have them give their youngster permission to leave.

A <u>Staff Safe Room</u> is a designated place for staff to go if they are having difficulty maintaining their composure in the classrooms. The room should have an element of privacy and be equipped with items such as tissues, writing materials, a teddy bear or two and refreshments such as juice and cookies. It should also contain information on typical reactions to crises and counseling benefits available through the district.

The Safe Room should be staffed by at least two people who are trusted by faculty and staff alike. Local mental health professionals, public safety chaplains or other outsiders often have implied credibility.

A mechanism for staff to be relieved of their duties for a few minutes needs to be in place prior to the event and should be discussed with all faculty/staff members during any before school briefing.

Parent/Community Informational Meeting

When an accident with serious injury hits a school community, it may be advisable to hold a Parent/Community Informational Meeting. This can reassure parents that the buses are safe and provide a means for other community members to express their concerns and get information.

The meeting can be held from as soon as a few days after the event to anytime within a couple of weeks. Arrange for translators, transportation and childcare if appropriate. The format of the meeting should be one that allows interaction and a forum to ask questions. Expect parents to be angry and scared. Allow that to be expressed appropriately. Encourage parents to talk with their children about their reactions. Also, inform the students that they may attend the meeting if they choose. Assure them that if they wish to speak, they will be heard.

A representative of the district's transportation department or the company handling the district's bus service should be at that meeting to answer questions and to provide reassurance. Local public safety and mental health professionals should also attend and play a large role. Police officers and firefighters can answer questions about the accident itself. Chaplains and mental health professionals can provide information on typical reactions to this type of event.

Anticipate that media will attend this meeting. Manage them by setting up interviews with key people ahead of time and giving them information on the program that will be presented. Also provide information on any and all steps the school district has taken before this event that emphasizes safety on buses.

Before School

When a serious accident affects your school community, a staff meeting before school is essential to share information and reactions. This meeting should be 30 to 60 minutes long and should be attended by all staff members: teachers, custodians, bus drivers, cafeteria workers, campus aides, etc. It should be organized by the Incident Management Team (who should have met prior to this meeting, at least by phone) and may be attended by local law enforcement or others to provide information and support.

The agenda should include general information on the accident and specific information about its aftermath. Of prime concern is identifying students and others who may be particularly vulnerable. Remind your staff that the reaction to a traumatic event may include regression, confusion, forgetfulness, stomach upsets, emotional outburst and isolation. Encourage staff members to be honest with students about their reactions but not to use students as a forum to process their own feelings. Students need to see healthy modeling of grief. They also need to feel that the significant adults in their lives are still in control.

You might also suggest postponing any test scheduled for that day. While maintaining the day's structure provides a feeling of comfort and safety, you should have a realistic and sympathetic expectation of student performance.

Staff members may need extra support during this time so they can deal with their own reactions and still be a healthy support for students. If a person is having a particularly tough time, provide whatever assistance he or she might need – maybe an additional classroom aide, a break from extracurricular responsibilities or a few days off. Don't expect your staff to function in a "business as usual" manner.

Of particular concern should be the bus drivers. Managers should meet with all of the bus drivers to provide them information and a place to begin processing their own reactions. Each one of them will be thinking, "That could have been me!" They also will watch very closely to see if the district stands behind the involved driver and offers assistance and support. The other drivers need to be assured that support is available for any of their drivers who need it.

The district should anticipate the desire of media to get interviews or statements from other bus drivers. Encourage drivers to refer all questions to the person serving in the role of Public Information Officer. Remember, whatever is said in the first 24 hours will create the general impression and theme of the incident. Watch out for those who may be less than circumspect and be very cautious not to prematurely speculate on cause.

Plan:

- Convene Incident Management Team

- Update information through law enforcement, hospital or family sources

- Appoint one or two team members to be family liaisons

- Conduct a staff informational meeting

- Invite cafeteria workers, playground aides, custodians, etc. to the staff informational meeting

Day One - First Period

The beginning of the day is the crucial time to commence rumor control. If we don't give students accurate information, they will create their own stories, details and theories. Their fiction is often much more extreme than reality. It isn't necessary to give graphic details, but it is important to give facts. In other words, telling students that "As you know, there was a bus accident yesterday afternoon and several of our students were injured and are still in the hospital. There is an investigation to find out what exactly happened and why. We will share information with you as we can," will help them deal with reality, not supposition and rumors.

The classroom is an ideal setting to discuss not only the incident but also normal reactions. In fact, high school students need a time and place to talk about their fears and reactions. The discussion should focus on reactions of the students and what they may experience as the result of the shock and trauma of the incident.

This is also the time to start determining which students may be more vulnerable and refer them to a counselor or the Incident Management Team.

Plan:

- In each classroom have a teacher or an IMT member read announcement that was prepared by Incident Management Team

- Allow students a chance to talk about their reactions

- Answer questions as honestly as you can

- Students unable to maintain in a supportive classroom environment should be given a pass to the Safe Room

- Tell students where extra help and support is available for the rest of the day

- Encourage students to be aware of each other and walk a classmate to an adult if they need help

- Encourage students to talk to their parents about their reactions

- Encourage students to write notes or make cards for anyone hospitalized or injured

- Ask young children to draw pictures of the accident and then talk about them

Rest of the Day

As uninjured children who were on the bus come to school, meet them to welcome them and give them a few minutes to talk about the accident. Have adults walk with them to their classrooms to deflect some of the attention and questions. Expect that other children will be very curious and the students who were on the bus will become the center of attention. If the student is able and wants to, you might give them two or three minutes to tell their classmates about the incident. If the students are still very shaken by the event, keep them in the office or somewhere while they regain their composure.

A bus accident will have a tremendous effect on the entire school. Keep in mind that children who are emotionally impacted by an event sometimes isolate themselves from others. They may hide in bathrooms, back closets or little-used hallways. Make sure you check these areas every 15 minutes.

If you decide to prepare a letter to go home for parents or guardians, there are a few things to keep in mind. First, explain what has happened, expressing appropriate sentiment for the victims (i.e., wishing the injured a speedy recovery or conveying condolences for a death). Next, provide information to parents about their children's possible reactions. Also include available community resources, including 24-hour phone numbers for assistance. Last, if you plan to hold a Parent Informational Night, give details or alert them that more information is to follow.

When preparing a letter, reassure parents and guardians that this was a very isolated incident and their children are safe when on the school bus. Be careful not to impede any police investigation that might still be in progress. Above all, be sensitive to the victims' families. Depending on the circumstances, be sensitive to the bus driver's family as well.

A staff meeting after school serves several purposes. First, it enables you to update the staff on the current status of events. Second, it lays the groundwork for the next day's response. Last, it lets staff members decompress after a very intense day.

The agenda needs to allow for time to ventilate. One structure is to organize into small groups (no more than 10 people each) and give them a chance to talk about what the worst part of the day was for them. Allow 20 minutes or so for this.

After that, bring everyone back into the large group to share information and begin to identify those students that may need some additional help dealing with the tragedy. This is a good place to involve community resources such as chaplains, clergy, public safety or mental health professionals to educate your staff members on typical reactions. Also share the latest information you may have about the investigation, injuries, funeral services, charitable donations, etc. Conclude the meeting by going over any schedule you may have devised for the next day.

Plan:

- Set up and staff Safe Rooms for both students and staff

- Collect information on typical trauma reactions and have available

- If counselors or a district psychologist come to assist, have them sign in and out

- Activate referral process for at-risk students

- Call Personnel and get information on insurance benefits for staff through Employee Assistance Program or other resources and have available for staff in the Safe Room

- Incident Management Team remains visible

- If there was a death, purchase a scrapbook for students and staff to write notes, draw pictures or add photographs to be given to the family in about two weeks

- Check bathrooms and out of the way places every 15 minutes

- Prepare a letter or statement to go home to parents

- Keep Superintendent informed throughout the day

- Do not release "high-risk" students from school to go home unless a parent has been contacted

- At the end of the school day contact victims' families, hospitals or others for updates

Things to Emphasize

The points to remember when dealing with a bus accident are:

- The illusion of guaranteed safety has been shattered. Staff, parents and students may be afraid that it could happen again

- Be sensitive to the fact that the bus driver and his or her family need support

- There will be an ongoing police investigation

- Help is available for anyone who is feeling vulnerable

- Create a way to say goodbye. A journal or a scrapbook works well

- The school staff members may be "secondary" victims. They need support too

- Give accurate information to reduce rumors

- Principal and other key team members begin hospital visitation to those who are injured

- Get injured student's parent's permission for classmates to visit at the hospital

There are several points to remember when dealing with a bus accident. One of them is that the illusion of safety has been shattered and students, staff and parents may be afraid it could happen again. Be sure to reassure your school community that it was an isolated event and the district is doing everything possible to guarantee it doesn't happen again.

The Principal or designated person should visit the hospital and speak to the victims and their families. Offer assistance and support. If students are going to want to visit their classmates in the hospital, be sure and ask the victims' parents and the hospital staff if that is all right. It may be helpful to talk with students at school about appropriate behavior when visiting the hospital and what to expect when they get there. Some hospitals may arrange for a specific room or location for friends to gather. Check with the hospital to see what they want to do.

Be sensitive to the fact that the bus driver and his or her family need support. The driver experienced a very traumatic incident and may need extra help to cope. If the driver was injured or killed, his or her family may need extra support because there may be a tendency to look for an easy answer and "blame the driver." The families of other drivers will also be aware that it could happen to their relative also. As the police investigation continues into the cause of the accident, the school needs to continue to cooperate and be prepared that the incident will stay fresh in everyone's mind.

Encourage everyone – students, staff and parents – to seek help if they are feeling overwhelmed or vulnerable. Provide a method of closure and a way to say goodbye. A journal or scrapbook that students and staff can create and then give to the family works well.

Things to Avoid

- Don't make announcements over the PA system. Do not do an assembly to give information. Do it in small groups, such as classrooms instead. Assign an Incident Team member to deliver news to each classroom

- If there was a death, do not do a memorial. Let the family do that through a funeral service

- Don't be afraid to talk about the event with students. They need to talk about it to reduce their own risk

- Do not ignore the warning signs of other students or staff

- Do not assume you can support your own. Bring in professional counselors to provide help

- Do not clean out the victims' lockers, reassign their desks or take down their artwork for at least a day or two. Make changes deliberately

Avoid making an announcement over the PA system or doing an assembly to give information. Assign an Incident Management Team member to deliver a message to each classroom so students and staff have the advantage of being in a small, familiar group as they hear the news and begin to talk about their reactions. Allowing students to talk about the event and their reactions to it reduces the risk of vulnerability for some students. In a major event, it is appropriate to tap into the expertise of professional counselors to assist your school system on the journey to recovery. Do not clean out the victims' lockers, reassign their desks or take down their artwork for a day or two. Give everyone a chance to adjust to the loss.

Plan:

- Do not do an assembly to give information. Do it in small groups, such as classrooms instead

- If there was a death do not do a memorial. Let the family do that through a funeral service

- Do not assume you can support your own. Bring in outsiders to help

Day 2

A short staff meeting before school may be appropriate on Day 2. It can be used to present new information such as updates on injuries, funeral arrangements and referral procedures for at-risk students. It is also a good time to inform staff of any new resources that are available. Also, remind staff that students will have a difficult time concentrating and remembering. It may be advisable to postpone tests for a few days.

If you opt to skip a morning staff meeting, it is a good idea to prepare and distribute a bulletin. The bulletin should thank all staff members for their care and concern, remind them to refer high-risk or vulnerable students to counselors, give some strategies for self-care and outline the plan for the day.

Plan:

- Notify staff of time and place of meeting

- Set up coffee

- Print any informational material you are going to distribute

- Arrange room

- Conduct meeting

- Begin arranging for Critical Incident Stress Management activities for students and/or staff

- Start planning Parent/Community Informational Night

- Make signs with a crisis line number listed and post throughout the school

- During first period, update students with any new information that is appropriate

- If students are planning to visit injured in the hospital, discuss proper etiquette

- Do classroom activities that encourage students to talk or express feelings and reactions

- Give students information on Safe Room and how to access it

- Check bathrooms, closets and hallways every 15 minutes.

- If a family has requested students or staff speak at a funeral service, hold a brief meeting of those people to discuss what is both expected and appropriate

- Begin talking with students about proper etiquette while at the funeral service or while viewing the body

- Contact the funeral home for information on viewing procedures and hours

Day 3

By the third day, the school community should be beginning to settle down into its normal routine. There may be students returning to school for the first time since the accident. Be sure to provide special support for them as they return. This might include talking with them about the incident and accompanying them as they go to their classrooms.

It's also possible that your normal routine may be interrupted by a funeral service on this day or one of the following days. On the day a service is held, make provisions for students to attend with their parents' permission. Arrange for substitutes for staff members who wish to attend. If the service is held in the morning, encourage everyone to come back to school for the afternoon. Expect an emotional day as everyone continues to deal with the accident. Use this time to encourage everyone to contribute to the scrapbook that will be given to the family

Plan:

- Check bathrooms, closets and hallways every 15 minutes

- Continue to provide ways for students to talk about their reactions

- Use stories and activities in classrooms that illustrate how many times we ride the bus and nothing happens

- Encourage students to talk to someone they trust

- Continue to monitor students for high-risk and refer if necessary

- Contact mental health or other professional and ask them to speak at the Parent/Community Informational Evening

- Use the PIO to notify parents of the Parent/Community Informational Evening through newsletters, radio, television, reader boards, announcements, etc.

Day 4

As the week progresses, your school may begin to appear normal again. Remember there is a big difference between APPEARING normal and BEING normal. Expect occasional outbursts of emotion.

Plan:

- Check bathrooms, closets and hallways every 15 minutes

- Continue to refer students who may seem at-risk

- Discontinue the Safe Room if students aren't using it

- Squelch rumors as they surface

- If you have students returning for the first time, support their transition back to school

Day 5

Plan:

- Continue to refer students who may seem at-risk

- Encourage staff and students to contribute to the scrapbook

- Squelch rumors as they surface

- If you have students returning for the first time, support their transition back to school

Day 6

Plan:

- If you have students returning for the first time, support their transition back to school

- Continue to refer students who may seem at-risk

Day 7

In this situation, it may be helpful to hold a Parent/Community Informational Evening. This is a mechanism to allow parents to express the underlying fear that their child is vulnerable. This meeting is also a way to provide information to parents on how to best support their own child as he or she recovers from this tragedy. Ask your mental health professionals to contribute. Let them talk about the complex issues of feeling vulnerable, what some warning signs of trouble might be and how to intervene.

Reassure the parents that the school is doing everything it can to help the students recover and thank them for their support. Have handouts listing typical reactions to trauma, a 24-hour crisis number and any other information that seems appropriate. Provide translators, transportation and childcare if appropriate.

Plan:

- Conduct a Parent Informational Meeting

- Prepare handouts for distribution at meeting

- Arrange for snacks and beverages

- When it's over, write thank-you notes to speakers and translators

First Month

During the first week or so, students and staff will talk a lot about the event. After a couple of weeks it will start to seem as though everyone has forgotten about it. The reality is that people are still thinking about it and each may believe he or she is the only one. Hopefully enough information was given in the beginning to help people understand that getting over a tragedy takes time. For some, the shock won't wear off for weeks or even months. Remind everyone that if they are having trouble sleeping, making decisions or eating, then they are experiencing normal reactions. Others are probably having similar reactions even though they may not be sharing their feelings. Most importantly, reassure all students and staff that they are not alone.

After the first couple of weeks, it's important to convey the message that it's still OK to talk about the incident. You might encourage teachers to bring up the subject every now and then. A teacher might say something like, "I've been thinking about the bus accident a lot the last couple of days and how scary that was. I'll bet some of you have been thinking about it too." This provides a forum to continue to talk about the trauma and feeling scared.

As victims are released from the hospital and return to school, expect an increase in critical incident stress. Plan for it and be prepared to manage it.

Also, expect that students may regress or try to cope inappropriately as a reaction to this accident. High school students are sometimes hesitant to talk about any reaction that they may perceive as being "weak." Reactions such as stomach upsets, bouts of tears, forgetfulness or headaches may be difficult for the students to discuss without some prompting. Adolescents may try to escape feelings by increased use of alcohol or other drugs, risky behavior or bravado acts. Teachers and parents can help just by being aware and encouraging healthy coping such as talking, exercising, good eating habits or any other form of expression that may be helpful. If a law enforcement investigation continues, each new development will again focus on the event. Allow that to take its natural rhythm and provide places for students and staff to vent feelings and emotions. Continue to provide information on typical reactions to grief or critical incident stress and resources that are available to help.

Beyond First Month

As time goes by, be aware of anniversaries or any other "trigger" events that might happen. If the accident occurred during a field trip, another field trip may trigger another reaction. If there was a death, the end of the school year will almost certainly trigger a reaction of some sort. As people say goodbye and look back over the year, the tragedy will be the topic of conversation again. The school must be prepared to allow students time and a mechanism to express that pain. If the students seem to be having trouble with this, a circulated yearbook that everyone can sign and then give to the family may be helpful. Allow your students to <u>do</u> something; it encourages closure.

Should a police investigation continue, expect the tragedy to become fresh with each new development. If someone is found to be at fault, the media attention will be intense. If a trial is held, those people closest to the event probably will have to testify. In many ways, this can become a second victimization. Expect to continue dealing with reactions for some time to come.

Plan:

- Continue to monitor reactions

- Conduct an evaluation of how the crisis was handled

- Make whatever changes are indicated to make your school safe again

- Update crisis plan as necessary

APPENDIX II

WERA Colloquium – March 6, 2017

Surviving or Thriving:
Educator Change Following a Traumatic School Experience

Mona M. Johnson, Ed.D.

Mona.m.johnson1@gmail.com

Overview: Situated in the Pacific Northwest, this qualitative study explored the coping, change, and systemic support experienced by thirteen K-12 educators following a school-based trauma. It is grounded in the theoretical framework of posttraumatic growth, the systematic study of how individuals are changed by traumatic encounters in positive ways. Participants in this study witnessed traumatic events—school shootings, physical assaults, or accidents resulting in the injury or death of a student or staff member--and were responsible as first responders to care for the life and death needs of others.

"So it was really busy afterwards, and I think for me, what I've learned about myself is probably dealing with the stress of what happened, the trauma of what happened…It was good for me to keep busy, because—and it's not that I didn't cry, but I couldn't cry because you had to go back to work and you had to hold it together."

Purpose: To understand what can be learned from K-12 educators who have survived school-based trauma through exploration of coping, change, and systemic support experienced following a traumatic event.

Research Questions and Themes:

1. How do educators **cope** following a school-based trauma? Themes included a focus on caring for others; a need to manage emotions; return to work routine; discomfort and need to reframe memories.

2. How do educators **change** following a school-based trauma? Themes included increased stress and rumination; need to seek support; emotional

reactions or triggers; confidence in dealing with future trauma; increased empathy

3. What systemic **supports** are available to help educators following a trauma? Themes included positive support from family, friends and colleagues; varying support from school administration; professional counseling; changes in personal belief systems.

4. What **advice** do these educators have for others who may experience a school based trauma? Themes included prepare for litigation; provide incident debriefing; practice emergency operations – including post trauma recovery planning; check in regularly; take care of yourself.

"I fell apart. It's like my body, I hit the rock bottom, my body hurt. I mean, I was in lots of pain and had headaches, and I had no energy, and then I found out I was depressed. I would say at that time it was all about finally finding help, going back to one of my providers and saying, "I need you to fix me. I am broken." I can't fix myself. I tried. I have been trying, and it's not working."

Findings:

1. Experiencing school-based traumatic events is as **horrific and difficult** for K-12 staff and faculty as it is for students.

2. The needs of K-12 educators who have experienced school-based trauma, regardless of courage or resilience, are **marginalized**.

3. K-12 educators need and deserve **ready-access to short- and long-term coping supports** in schools following trauma

4. Educators, in particular school and district leaders, lack capacity to fully understand the impact of trauma on school systems and strategies to integrate trauma-informed practices into their daily workplace interactions.

5. Traumatic experiences cause **anguish** but **can also lead to positive growth** in the presence of authentic and compassionate systemic supports.

6. Recovery from trauma is **a long term process requiring active and collective involvement** of trauma survivors, family, friends, colleagues, schools and the community.

Barbara J. Ertl, MS, LPC, NCC & Dr. Mary Schoenfeldt

"After the initial incident, no one from the district did ever talk to me. I just think I was a liability to them. They were in the middle of a lawsuit and I was a liability— I don't know how I could have been. I didn't feel like I was in that circle of support."

Recommendations:

1. Further **explore impacts of school-based trauma** on educators including the differential impacts of trauma and systemic supports needed to enhance coping for educators **beyond the Pacific Northwest**.

2. Examine and identify **best-practices and posttraumatic incident response strategies** to minimize the short- and long-term personal and professional impacts on educators.

3. Further **assess theoretical implications** of posttraumatic growth on K-12 educators coping with the aftermath of school-based trauma.